HISTORIC PHOTOS OF
USC FOOTBALL

TEXT AND CAPTIONS BY STEVE SPRINGER

TURNER
PUBLISHING COMPANY

This 1905 squad was led by USC's first paid coach, Harvey Holmes, and played for the first time against a major college. The opponent was Stanford and the result was disappointing for USC, a 16–0 defeat. Included in its 6-3-1 record were victories over Whittier Reform School, a national guard team, and the USC alumni.

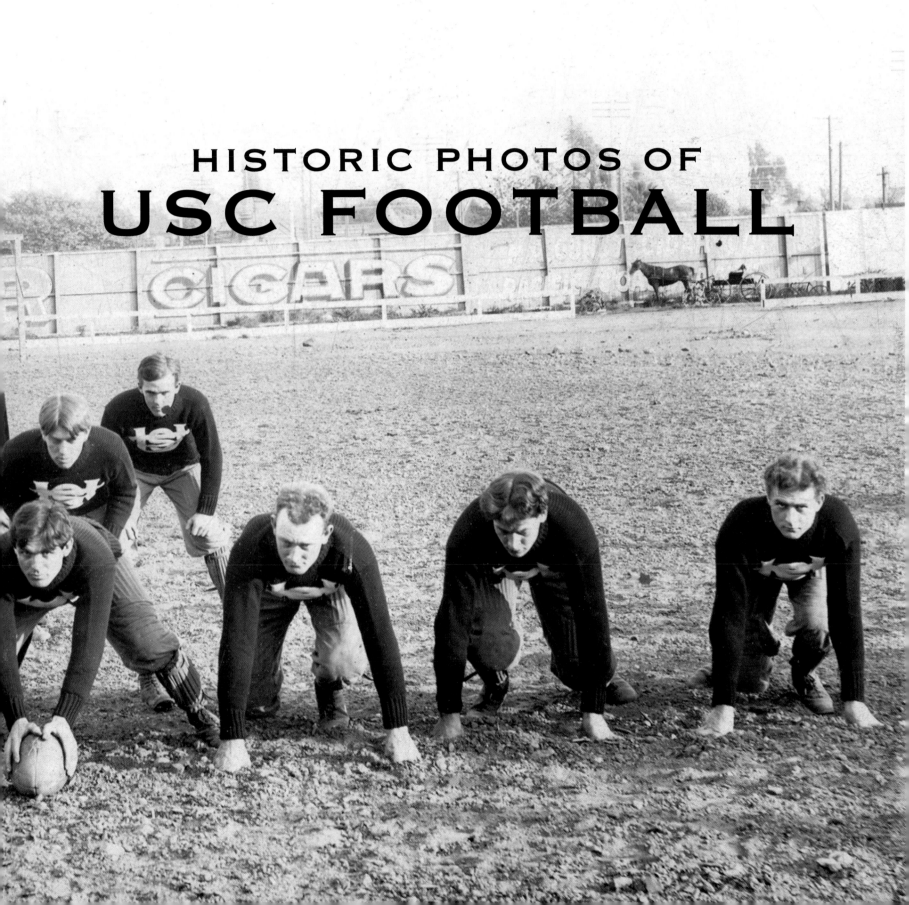

HISTORIC PHOTOS OF
USC FOOTBALL

Turner Publishing Company
200 4th Avenue North • Suite 950
Nashville, Tennessee 37219
(615) 255-2665

www.turnerpublishing.com

Historic Photos of USC Football

Copyright © 2010 Turner Publishing Company

Library of Congress Control Number: 2009939392

ISBN: 978-1-59652-571-9

Printed in China

10 11 12 13 14 15 16—0 9 8 7 6 5 4 3 2 1

CONTENTS

Here is a 1913 rugby match against Manual Arts High School. "We are looking for a foothold on an athletic ladder that would carry us, we hoped, to a level of competition to the proportion of our ambitious, restless, growing young institution," said a USC spokesman in explaining the switch to rugby in *The Trojan Heritage* by Mal Florence.

ACKNOWLEDGMENTS

This book would not have been possible without the help of the University of Southern California and Tim Tessalone, USC Sports Information Director. His vast knowledge and diligent effort was invaluable in identifying the people and events in some of these photographs.

Also invaluable were

The Trojan Heritage by Mal Florence (Jordan & Company, Publishers, 1980)

Fight On by Steve Bisheff and Loel Schrader (Cumberland House, 2006)

60 Years of USC-UCLA Football by Steve Springer and Michael Arkush (Longmeadow Press, 1991)

The Rose Bowl Media Guide, produced by the Pacific-10 Conference public relations department (2002)

Spaulding's Official Rugby Football Guide, 1914, ed. Joseph R. Hickey (American Sports Publishing Co.)

Traditionally Yours, Arnold Eddy (1988)

Fanbase.com

College Football Historical Society

Research Journals Archive, Jim McGreal

Collier's Magazine

PREFACE

In a field once covered with mustard seed near downtown Los Angeles, a college football program sprouted in the late 1880s and grew as did so many others across the nation. Growth was in spurts. That growth can be seen from a unique viewpoint through the nearly 200 photos in this book that are spread over nearly 100 years.

What began with young men adorned with handlebar mustaches seeking a respite from studies at the new University of Southern California was elevated into formal play in 1888. Some of the initial competition would be laughable today, consisting of high schools and athletic clubs. It wasn't even football as it is now played. A touchdown was worth four points, a field goal five. Tackling below the waist was a foul.

For three years (1911-13), USC gave up football altogether. With the sport castigated for its violence, and the University of California and Stanford abandoning their programs to concentrate on rugby, USC did the same. But in 1914, football returned to the university and, in less than a decade, soared from a unique form of exercise to a focal point of the campus. Led by Elmer "Gloomy Gus" Henderson—his nickname derived from his tendency to belittle his players—the Trojans arrived on the national stage. They played in their first Rose Bowl, and moved from cozy Bovard Field (capacity 12,000) to the mammoth Los Angeles Memorial Coliseum, where 100,000 fans could be crammed in.

What followed in the ensuing decades would have been enough to turn Gloomy Gus into Happy Henderson. Under coaches like Howard Jones, John McKay, and John Robinson, there were national championships, Heisman Trophy winners, an endless stream of All-Americans, and so many trips to the Rose Bowl on New Year's Day that USC's appearance in that showcase football showdown became almost as predictable as the Rose Parade itself.

But whether the Trojans made it to the Rose Bowl or not, they had another big showdown every year. There are fierce rivalries all across the college football landscape, but in terms of history, geography, and tradition, nothing quite matches USC–Notre Dame. Begun in 1926, this annual confrontation has made or ruined seasons, cost jobs, and established reputations. If Anthony Davis had never gained another yard for USC, scoring 11 touchdowns against the Fighting Irish assured him an honored place in Trojan lore. If Johnny Baker had never kicked a football again, his game-winning field goal against Notre Dame in 1931 was enough to make him a USC hero for the ages.

For a long time, the Trojans ruled L.A. in terms of team sports. There were no Rams, Raiders, Dodgers, or Lakers to intrude on their turf. And UCLA, the other university in town, couldn't match USC's football accomplishments. The only competitor was the Pacific Coast League with the Los Angeles Angels and Hollywood Stars sharing L.A. But popular as they were, those teams were in a minor league competing against a national powerhouse. When USC beat Notre Dame in South Bend in 1931 to end the 26-game unbeaten streak of the Fighting Irish, the Trojans were welcomed home by 300,000 fans lining the streets for their parade.

The focal point widened after World War II. The Rams arrived in L.A. to huge crowds of their own, the Dodgers briefly invaded the Coliseum and soon took over the town during baseball season, the Raiders had their moments in the Coliseum, the Lakers and John Wooden's Bruins made basketball prime entertainment, and the Kings made a splash in the years when they had Wayne Gretzky. But USC held firm to its fan base. Cardinal and gold has remained as prominent as Dodger blue and Laker purple and gold. Saturday afternoons are still Trojan time.

Their marching band has played all over the world. Their players have ranged from the famous (such as Marion Morrison, better known as the film star John Wayne) to the infamous (O. J. Simpson). More than 400 USC players have gone on to pro football, including 11 who reached the Pro Football Hall of Fame. Some of the NFL's most familiar figures, from Al Davis to Joe Gibbs, got their start coaching at USC.

Now in its second century, L.A.'s oldest team remains as vital as ever. Especially to those directly involved. No matter where they go in life, former Trojans retain their loyalty. Like Mal Florence, who went on to a long, distinguished career as a sportswriter for the *Los Angeles Times*. When it came to his old university, his objectivity wavered. Florence once wrote a coffee-table book about USC football titled *The Trojan Heritage*. Asked why he didn't write a similar coffee-table book about UCLA football, Florence replied with a grin, "They don't make coffee tables that small."

—Steve Springer

Founded in 1880, the University of Southern California fielded its first official football team, shown here, in 1888 and went undefeated that season. It wasn't much of a season—only two games. Both against the Alliance Athletic Club. USC won the first game 16–0, and the second 4–0. Frank Suffel (second from the right in the top row) and Henry Goddard (not pictured) were the player-coaches.

FROM VACANT LOTS TO RUGBY FIELDS

(1880s–1918)

It began in obscurity. Eleven college students in padded vests on a vacant lot taking on the Los Angeles Y.M.C.A. in a game that had become popular on the East Coast, a game called football. It was the mid-1880s and the students were from the University of Southern California, founded in 1880 and built on ground where mustard plants once grew.

By 1888, USC had kicked off its first official football season. Sort of. The team, coached by Henry Goddard and Frank Suffel, played two games against the Alliance Athletic Club and won them both, 16–0 and 4–0. In 1889, USC faced its first college, St. Vincent's (later known as Loyola Marymount), and won 40–0. The fulfillment of visions of grandeur, however, was still a long way off. A decade later, USC couldn't beat Los Angeles High School, winding up with a loss and a tie in two meetings in 1898.

USC got its first paid coach, Harvey Holmes, in 1904. A year later, his team faced its first university, Stanford, and lost 16–0. Credibility for USC, muddled in controversy, would not come easily. There were accusations of bending eligibility rules and a charge in 1904 that team captain Dan Caley had been secretly paid 25 dollars. The bigger threat was to the sport itself, perceived by many as being too violent. When the University of California and Stanford both dropped football and switched to rugby, USC, anxious to emulate its big brothers to the north, did the same from 1911 to 1913. The only memorable moment from those years came on February 24, 1912, when *Los Angeles Times* sportswriter Owen R. Bird referred to the team as the Trojans. The name stuck. Rugby didn't.

Football returned to USC in 1914 on a grander scale than before. On the roster, university opponents began to elbow aside the athletic clubs and high schools USC had faced in earlier years. In 1919, Elmer "Gloomy Gus" Henderson assumed the helm as head coach of the Trojans. He brought with him innovative practices like aggressive recruiting and ideas like the spread formation. His nickname came about because of his tendency to denigrate his own players to the media. But there was nothing gloomy about the results on the field. Gloomy Gus would usher in a bright new era for USC football.

There's a reason Lewis Freeman, the man in the middle of the back row in this 1897 team photo, is the only one wearing a tie. He was USC's first non-playing football coach. He also served as equipment manager, supplying the team with its uniforms. USC won five of its six games that season, losing only to the San Diego Y.M.C.A., 18–0.

The uniforms looked sharper a year later, and the team, known as the Methodists or Wesleyans in those days, remained nearly as sharp on the field, going 5-1-1. The loss (6–0) and the tie (0–0) both came against Los Angeles High School, a team that also beat several other universities.

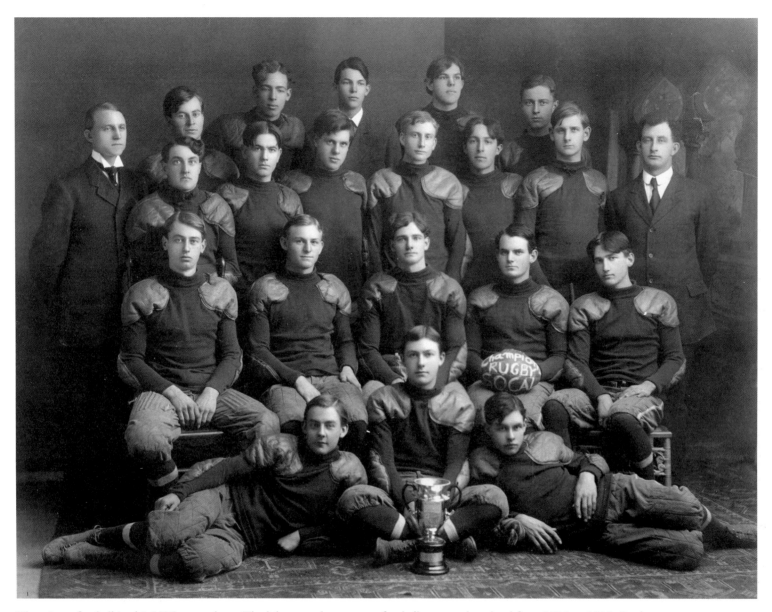

There is no football in this USC team photo. That's because there was no football team at the school from 1911 to 1913. Rugby had become a leading sport at the University of California and Stanford, so USC, anxious to remain a meaningful athletic force, joined the crowd. Bad idea. The Trojans lost both on the field and at the box office. The rugby ball, visible in the photograph, is rounder than a football and has no laces.

This is the 1912 USC rugby team. This season had a lasting impact on the college, one that continues to this day. And it had nothing to do with what occurred on the field. On February 24, 1912, writing in the *Los Angeles Times,* sportswriter Owen R. Bird gave the USC players the nickname "Trojans."

The 1913 USC rugby team looks out of place in this peaceful setting. Matched against California, Stanford, the Los Angeles Athletic Club, and All Blacks, a New Zealand squad, USC finished 4-3-2. In their most humiliating defeat, the Trojans lost to All Blacks 40–0.

USC plays California in a 1913 rugby match. The Trojans opened the season by beating the Cal freshmen 6–0. But in a matchup of the two varsity squads in the season finale for the Trojans, Cal and USC played to a 3–3 tie. California finished up with three games against All Blacks, losing all three by a combined score of 102–3.

This is USC's rugby team in action. The stands in the background are nearly deserted, an all-too-familiar sight for the sport. Failure to generate a strong program and a strong fan base drove USC back to football after three seasons.

The day is September 26, 1914, and football has returned to USC, not to disappear again. With Ralph Glaze as head coach, the Trojans made it a triumphant comeback, beating the Los Angeles Athletic Club 20–0. At least one thing hadn't changed. A year earlier, USC and the LAAC were battling each other on the rugby field and the Trojans were dominant there as well, going 3-1-1 in their five meetings.

Here's a closer view of the 1914 USC–Los Angeles Athletic Club game, played at Bovard Field, named for USC president George F. Bovard. This game marked not only the return of football, but the return of a rival USC had last faced in this sport in 1896. In that earlier game, played in front of 1,500 at L.A.'s Athletic Park, LAAC won 22–0.

USC repeated its domination in its second game of 1914, shown here in a 41–0 victory over Redlands. That gave the Trojans a cumulative score of 61–0 in their opening two games. But the euphoria faded after a 3-0 start when they lost three of their final four.

Another photo of USC vs. Redlands in 1914. The Trojans had a rougher time when they traveled to Redlands later in the season, but still won, 13–6. This season included USC's initial trip outside California. The Trojans went to Tacoma, Washington, where they lost to Oregon State, 38–6.

Revving up for the 1915 season. It would be an ambitious year for the Trojans with California, Oregon, St. Mary's, and Utah on their schedule. Ultimately, however, it would be a losing season, USC finishing at 3 wins, 4 losses.

This goal-line struggle is between USC and the Los Angeles Athletic Club in the Trojans' 1915 season opener at Bovard Field.
USC repeated its victory of a year earlier over LAAC, winning this time 21–9.

This is more action from the 1915 USC-LAAC game. It was the beginning of the second and final season for Trojan head coach Ralph Glaze, who played his college football at Dartmouth, played end on the 1905 All-American team, and briefly pitched for the Boston Red Sox alongside a teammate named Cy Young.

The 1915 Trojans play St. Mary's at Bovard Field. In the ensuing decades, St. Mary's would grow into a national powerhouse, but, on this day, they were crushed 47–3. St. Mary's would get its revenge as it got better, winning four of its next eight games against USC.

USC closed out the 1915 season with this game against Whittier, a game the Trojans lost 20–2. It was played at a neutral site, Washington Park, located at Washington and Hill in downtown Los Angeles.

USC opened its 1916 season with a 14–0 victory at home against the Sherman Institute of Riverside. Home for the Trojans for that season was Fiesta Park, located at Pico Boulevard and Grand Avenue, another downtown L.A. site.

Having won their first two games of the 1916 season, against a high school and an athletic club, by a combined score of 28–0, the Trojans are shown here preparing for their first university opponent, Utah. The difference was humbling, USC losing 27–12 in front of 2,000 at Fiesta Park.

A crowd of 10,000 turned out at Fiesta Park for USC's 1916 game against Cal. It was a disappointing day for the Trojan fans, as Cal soared to a 27–0 victory.

Dr. George F. Bovard, president of USC, is shown in the foreground, working the crowd. The fourth president in the university's history—he followed his brother Marion M. Bovard, Joseph P. Widney, and George W. White—Bovard served from 1903 to 1921.

After getting walloped by two universities, Utah and Cal, the 1916 Trojans returned to the club level and beat the Los Angeles Athletic Club, in a game shown here, 34–0. That didn't do much to quiet the doubts about Coach Dean Cromwell, starting his second tour of duty with USC.

Here are the 1916 Trojans finally beating a college, though not a major university, defeating Pomona 28–3 at Fiesta Park. The knock on Cromwell was that his expertise was in track and field, where he won a dozen NCAA titles, not in football.

In this 1916 photo, the crowd watches USC lose to Oregon State 16–7. The Trojans would close out their season with a 20–7 win over Arizona in Phoenix, enabling Cromwell to finish with a winning record at 5-3. He had chalked up a cumulative 10-1-3 as USC's coach in 1909-10.

Back in the familiar surroundings of Bovard Field, the Trojans are shown opening the 1917 season as they concluded the previous year, with a victory over Arizona. The score this time was 31–6, but the mood was very different. The United States had entered World War I, depleting the ranks of college football and inspiring thoughts of battle on a far more dangerous field.

The 1917 Trojans are shown doing their part for the war effort by giving the U.S. Army a game and its troops a workout. Playing the Twenty-first Infantry squad down in San Diego in front of a crowd of 5,000, USC won 3–0.

The 1917 Trojans played two more games against teams from the military. USC hosted a squad from Fort MacArthur and trounced the visitors 42–0. It took the Marines to finally bring USC down. Here, the Mare Island Marines beat the Trojans 34–0 at Washington Park in L.A.

This 1917 game seemed to have everything. There were the festivities of Thanksgiving Day, a crowd of 10,000 at Bovard Field, and a traditional rival, Cal, across the line of scrimmage from the Trojans. The only thing missing were points on the scoreboard. The two teams played to a 0–0 tie.

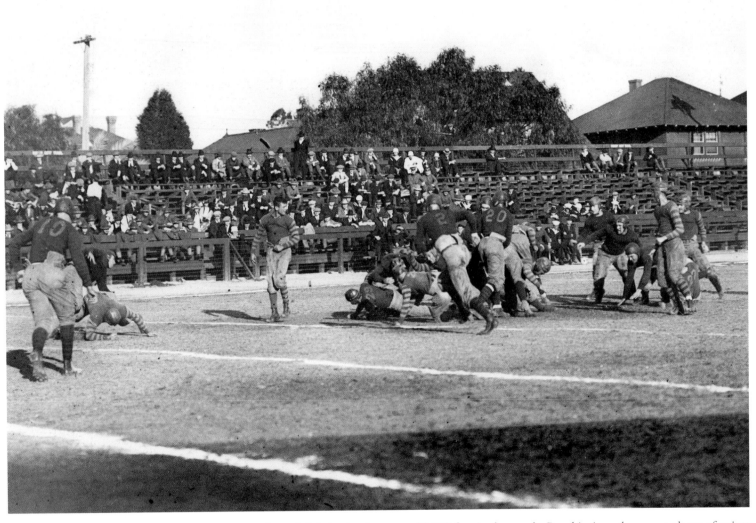

Again in 1918, USC hosted Cal. Again, there were 10,000 fans in the stands. But this time, there were plenty of points on the scoreboard, far more than USC would have liked. Cal won 33–7. A disturbing pattern was evolving for USC. After losing to the Trojans in their first meeting in 1915, Cal enjoyed a nine-game unbeaten streak against its southern rivals, consisting of eight wins and a tie.

Although it wasn't officially counted as a game, USC played a team from a submarine base in San Pedro in 1918, winning 34–0. The empty stands in the background tell a bigger story about that season. The 1918 Spanish influenza epidemic, which took the lives of 50 million people worldwide, resulted in a ban of public gatherings in October, forcing USC to delay its season opener until late November. The virus was unusual in that it hit young adults hardest, and among the sick were many members of the team.

THUNDER ACROSS THE NATION

(1919–1940)

He came from Broadway High School in Seattle, hardly known as a launching pad for collegiate coaching careers. By the time Elmer C. "Gloomy Gus" Henderson was finished coaching USC however, he had launched the Trojans into the national spotlight, into a place of prominence among college football's elite that they would forever maintain.

After Henderson's third season, USC was admitted into the Pacific Coast Conference. In his fourth season, Henderson put the Trojans in their first Rose Bowl, where they played Penn State and won 14–3. A year later, USC had a stadium to match its rising aspirations, moving from Bovard Field (capacity 12,000) to the Los Angeles Memorial Coliseum, where the Trojans would eventually draw in excess of 100,000 spectators on several occasions.

If Henderson had a flaw, it was his failure to beat northern rival California. Some say Henderson's 0-5 record against Cal was the reason he was fired after the 1924 season. Others blame it on a feud that pitted USC against Stanford and Cal over unsubstantiated charges that USC had questionable recruiting practices and academic standards. Whatever the reason, Henderson, despite a 45-7 record over six seasons, was gone, leaving a big hole to fill.

Howard Jones was picked to try. He not only perpetuated the upward arc Henderson had charted for the Trojans, but he took USC to the ultimate peak, winning a national championship not once, but three times in his 16 years as head coach. That is, as the Headman, as he was known.

Jones took the team to five Rose Bowls, won them all, and packed his rosters with the school's first 19 All-Americans. It was on his watch that USC's storied rivalry with Notre Dame began. Jones' focus on the running game and the steely determination of coach and players caused his teams to be named the Thundering Herd. The highlight of his reign may have been the 16–14 victory over Notre Dame at South Bend in 1931, ending a 26-game unbeaten streak by the Fighting Irish. Jones and his team came home to a parade, the spectators 300,000 strong.

Then it all ended with alarming suddenness. On July 27, 1941, Jones suffered a heart attack and died. He was 55. He left behind a 121-36-13 record and an unprecedented list of achievements. Who would drive the Herd now?

Elmer "Gloomy Gus" Henderson addresses his players in 1919, the first of his six seasons as USC's head coach. It would prove to be a very successful six seasons. Taking over for Dean Cromwell, who was 2-2-2 in his final year, Henderson's Trojans would finish 4-1 in 1919, and 45-7 over his six seasons at the helm.

USC plays Occidental in 1919 in Henderson's second game. The Trojans would win 27–0, after beating Pomona 6–0 in Henderson's debut. Despite his players' success, Henderson was known for criticizing them, thus earning the nickname "Gloomy Gus."

USC plays one of its favorite opponents, Cal Tech, to open the 1920 season at Bovard Field. In its 13 meetings against the Trojans ending in 1927, Cal Tech eked out one win and one tie, both in the 1890s. USC won this game 46–7, part of a string of eight straight victories over Cal Tech by a combined score of 335–20.

The 1920 Trojans face another favorite opponent, Occidental. USC won 48–7, part of a ten-game winning streak against Occidental. Victory and dominance were the norm for the Trojans that season. They finished 6-0, outscoring the opposition 170–21.

USC moves toward victory during the 1920 USC-Occidental game. Despite the Trojan triumphs, Henderson continued to earn his Gloomy Gus nickname. He once told Paul Lowry, an *L.A. Times* sportswriter, that USC's line would make swiss cheese blush and that his center was the center of gloom.

How would the 1920 Trojans do against a major university? This game against Oregon and a game earlier in the season against Stanford answered the doubters. The Trojans beat Stanford 10–0 and won this game, played at Tournament Park in Pasadena, 21–0.

This 1920 USC-Oregon game, played in front of 20,000 on Thanksgiving Day, was the beginning of a period of such dominance in this series that to call it a rivalry would be charitable. Not only did USC go unbeaten in ten straight games with nine wins and a tie, but the Trojans shut out Oregon in the first six of those games, winning by a combined score of 192–0.

The guns of World War I had long since fallen silent by 1921, but that didn't stop USC from continuing to schedule games with armed forces teams. Here the Trojans battle one of three military opponents, none of whom scored in four games. USC beat teams from the USS *Arizona* (62–0), USS *New York* (35–0,) and a squad from a San Pedro submarine base twice (34–0 and 28–0).

The Trojans are shown playing on Occidental's field. That didn't slow USC in its march to a six-game, unbeaten and unscored-upon start to the 1921 season. Since four of those games were against service teams and one was against Cal Tech, Occidental was the best of that group. No matter. USC won 42–0.

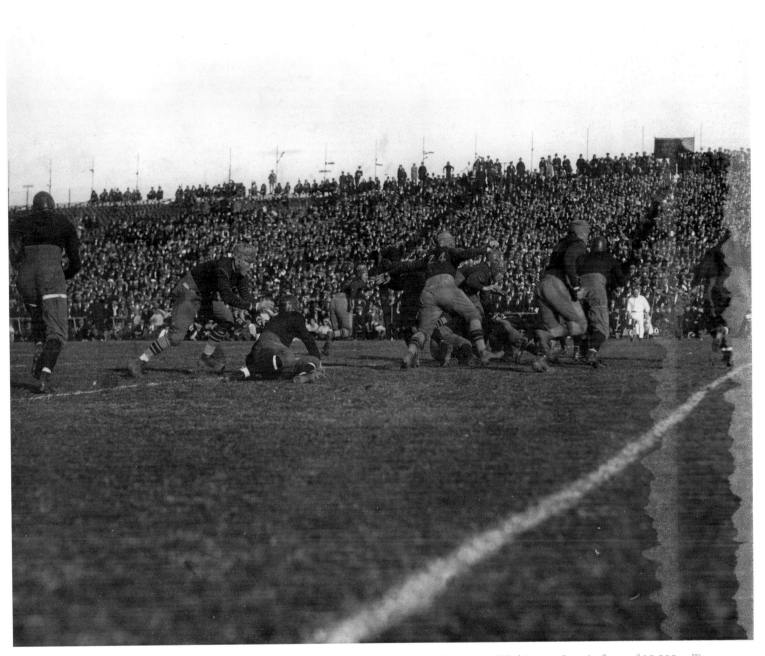

The Trojans are shown closing out their 1921 season with a 28–7 victory over Washington State in front of 18,000 at Tournament Park in Pasadena. Under Henderson, USC developed its first four All-Americans: quarterback–running back Morley Drury, running back Mort Kaer, guard Brice Taylor, and tackle Jesse Hibbs.

A sing-along breaks out at a Trojan practice. They might be singing "Fight On," the music composed by USC dental student
Milo Sweet in 1922, or "All Hail," music and lyrics by Al Wesson, a member of the Trojan Marching Band, for the finale of the
1923 campus show "Conquest."

Here is the most famous person ever to come out of the USC football program. Certainly not because of his accomplishments on the field. Because of a surfing accident, he never had the chance to advance beyond a reserve role, ultimately having to leave the university when his injuries led to cancellation of his football scholarship. His name was Marion Morrison. The world would come to know him as John Wayne.

Morrison, shown here standing in the background at center, enrolled at USC for the 1925 season, but as a freshman he was ineligible to play for the varsity. Morrison did play as a reserve in 1926, but by 1927, his scholarship had been dropped by his coach, Howard Jones, because of the surfing injury. Morrison left school just as talkies were about to revolutionize the movie business. And Morrison's life.

This is USC in 1922 in its final season at cozy Bovard Field where the capacity was 12,000. In 1923, the Trojans moved to the Los Angeles Memorial Coliseum where the first game, against Pomona, exceeded Bovard's best by drawing 12,863.

This is New Year's Day 1923, a momentous occasion for USC as it makes its first appearance in the Rose Bowl game. It was also the first time this New Year's Day showdown was played in the new Rose Bowl stadium. Before 1923, the game had been held in nearby Tournament Park. The Trojans beat Penn State 14–3 to finish the season 10–1.

Gloomy Gus Henderson doesn't look so gloomy here, smiling for a photographer. However, the USC coach would have reason to be gloomy a year after this 1923 photograph. Unable to beat Cal, and hit with charges of questionable recruiting by Stanford and Cal, charges that were never substantiated, Henderson was fired after the 1924 season.

A crowd of 43,000 watches USC beat Penn State in the Rose Bowl, so named because of its bowl shape. This New Year's Day game, initially played in 1902, was the first of the bowl games. All that followed used the word "bowl" to signify that they too offered a season-ending showdown. Even pro football with the Super Bowl.

The Trojans pose before the 1923 Rose Bowl. The USC squad was alone not only here, but in the pregame warm-up as well. The game was scheduled for a 2:15 kickoff, but when the time came, Penn State still hadn't arrived. Turned out, the Nittany Lions were caught in a traffic jam. The game started about an hour late.

In a photo taken at halftime of the 1923 Rose Bowl, the man on the left outside the railing holding a black hat is Rufus von KleinSmid, USC's fifth president. He held the position from 1921 to 1947. In the background are the white-shirted members of the Trojan rooting section.

With an 8-2 record, but only a 2-1 conference mark that left them tied for fourth, there was no Rose Bowl for the Trojans in 1924. So instead of playing on New Year's Day, USC played on Christmas Day in an event, shown here, named the Christmas Festival. The opponent, Missouri, was beaten by USC 20–7. It proved to be Henderson's last game as coach.

The Trojans practice under new coach Howard Jones. As the most successful coach in USC history, Jones not only filled Coach Henderson's shoes, he marched the team to an even higher level of achievement. Over 16 seasons, Jones led the Trojans to three national championships, an equal number of undefeated seasons, and five Rose Bowls, all of which the Trojans won.

This is Brice Taylor, a 5-foot-9, 185-pound guard who was not only USC's first All-American, but the school's first African-American player as well. What was truly amazing was his ability to successfully grapple with opposing linemen even though he was born without a left hand.

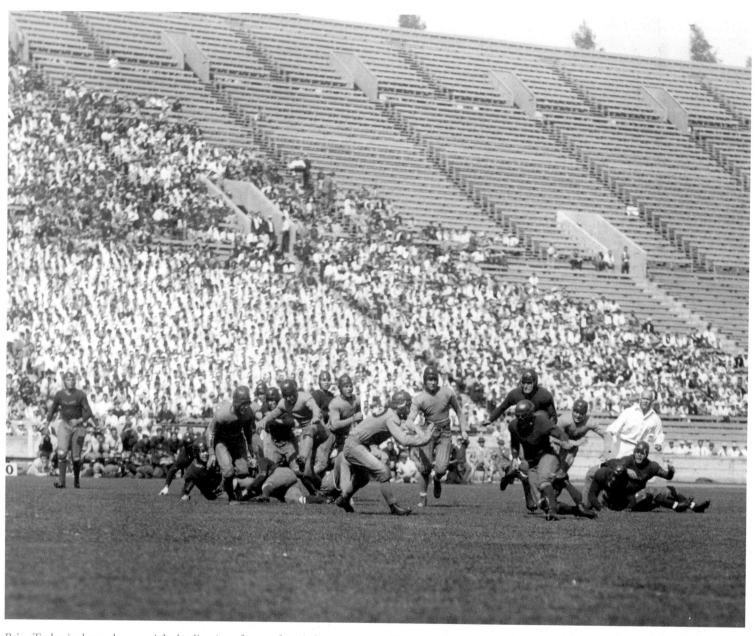

Brice Taylor is shown here at right leading interference for a ball carrier in a 1925 game. USC was 28-6 with Taylor, who was a Trojan for three seasons (1924-26). He was also a sprinter and hurdler on the USC track squad and a member of the mile relay team that recorded a world-record time.

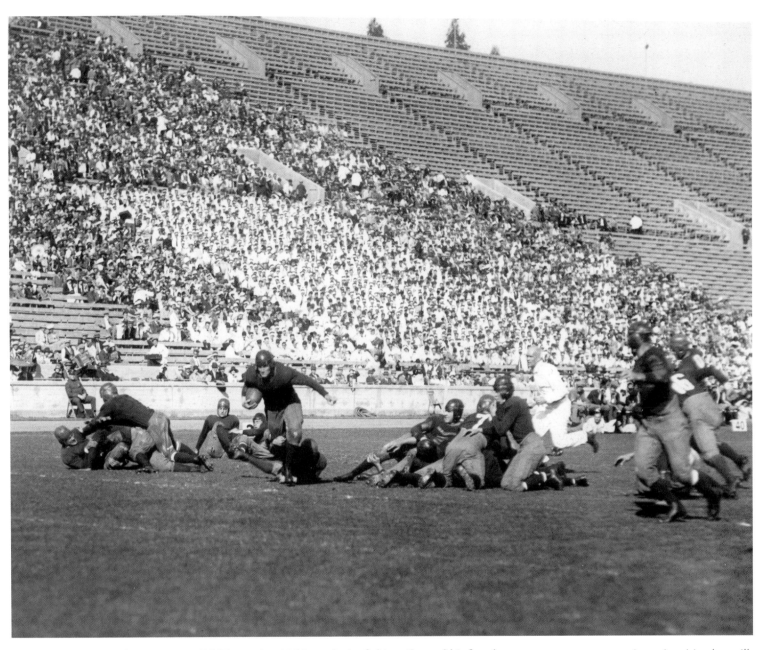

The Jones era at USC began in 1925 in explosive fashion. Granted his first three opponents were not major universities, but still, the scores inspired the faithful and intimidated the opposition. The Trojans beat Whittier 74–0, Cal Tech 32–0, and Pomona, in the game shown here, an eyebrow-raising 80–0.

In front of 66,000 at the Coliseum, the 1925 Trojans shut out Iowa 18–0. Jones's offense featured a dominating running game, his favorite play being a power sweep off right tackle. After a while, teams knew it was coming, but they still couldn't stop it.

This is Mort Kaer, who started a tradition of excellence at USC by becoming the school's first All-American tailback. In 1925, Kaer's second season and his first as the key figure in Jones' rushing attack, Kaer scored 114 points, the highest total in the nation. He also rushed for 576 yards. Kaer is a member of the National Football Foundation College Football Hall of Fame.

The 1926 Trojans face Washington State at the Coliseum in front of 34,700. USC won the game 16–7. The Trojans had never had an All-American when Jones arrived. By the time he left, 20 players had been so honored.

The 1926 Trojans beat Occidental 28–6 in front of 22,000 at the Coliseum. USC would finish the season 8-2, including a 5-1 conference mark. That was good for second place, the highest finish for the Trojans in their five years in the Pacific Coast Conference.

USC tailback Mort Kaer is shown struggling for extra yards against Stanford at the Coliseum in a 1926 game. The Trojans lost 13–12 in front of a capacity crowd of 78,500, the largest to see a USC game to that point. Kaer would go on to rush for 852 yards and score 72 points that season.

This is a 1927 photo of Jesse Hibbs, the college's first two-time All-American. Hibbs, team captain in 1928, also played basketball for the Trojans. He spent the 1931 season as a member of the Chicago Bears and then became a movie and television director.

It's practice time for the 1927 Trojans. Although Jones could be demanding as a coach, he never voiced those demands through profanity. "Gad darn it" was his strongest use of the language, according to *The Trojan Heritage*.

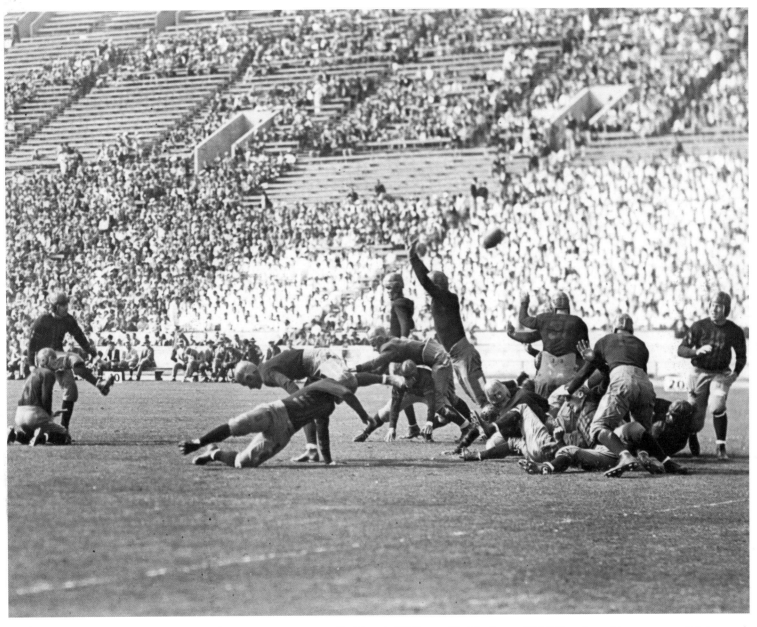

The Trojans open the 1927 season against Occidental. USC won 33–0 in front of 20,000 and would go on to an 8-1-1 record, including their first undefeated mark in the conference. At 4-0-1, they would finish in a first-place tie for the PCC title, but the co-champion, Stanford, would be selected for the Rose Bowl.

A gag shot of Jesse Hibbs in 1927, perhaps demonstrating how he helped drive the Trojans down the field. A year later, with Hibbs serving as team captain, USC would win its first national championship. The Trojans were 25-3-2 in Hibbs' three seasons on the team.

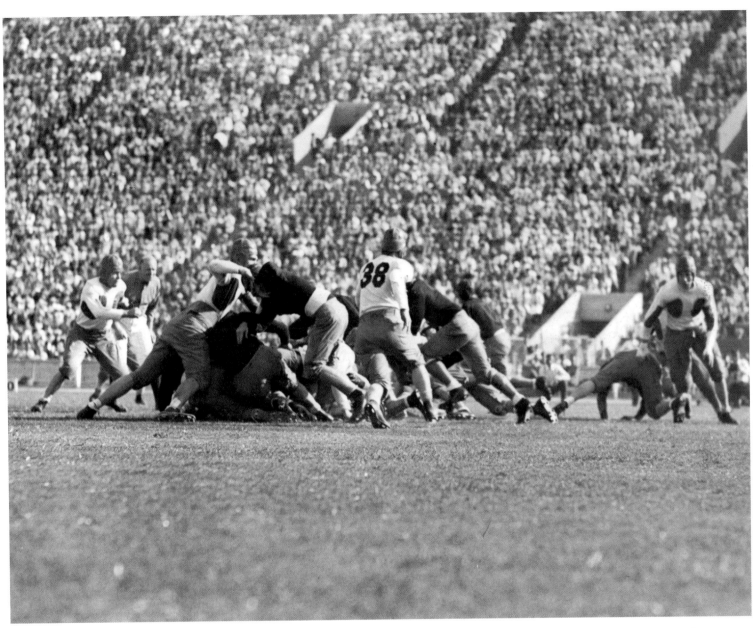

USC is shown playing Oregon State in 1927 at the Coliseum in front of 35,000. The Trojans won 13–12, part of a ten-game winning streak against the Beavers. Along the Coliseum sidelines that season galloped a white horse, ridden by a fan named Louis Shields and owned by a local banker. It was the start of a tradition that led to Traveler, the Trojan mascot who gallops to this day.

USC plays at Stanford in a 1927 game that would end in a 13–13 deadlock. The Trojans were lucky to escape with a tie after blowing a six-point lead with 30 seconds to play. Stanford scored on a three-yard pass from Herb Fleishhacker to Louis Vincenti, but kicker Mike Murphy missed the extra point.

Shown on the right is All-American Morley Drury. Called "the noblest Trojan of them all" by sportswriter Mark Kelly, Drury, a running back-quarterback-safety, was USC's first inductee into the National Football Foundation College Football Hall of Fame.

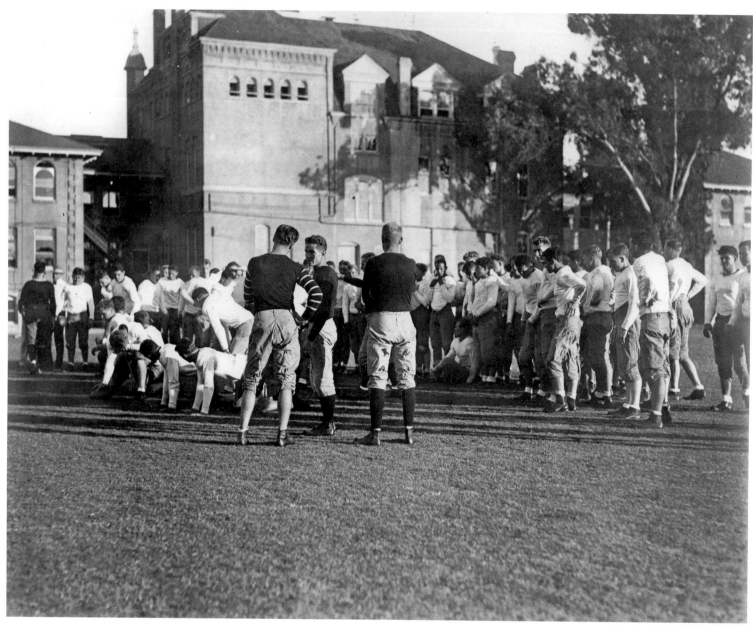

The 1928 Trojans sweat through another day of practice. It turned out to be well worth the effort. Under Jones, this team would go on to an undefeated season (9-0-1 including 4-0-1 in conference), culminating with its first national championship.

These Trojans are five of the 1928 national champions. On the top row, right to left, are halfback Lloyd Thomas, All-American quarterback Don Williams, and an unidentified teammate. Kneeling, right to left, are end Lawrence McCaslin and tackle Jesse Hibbs, another All-American.

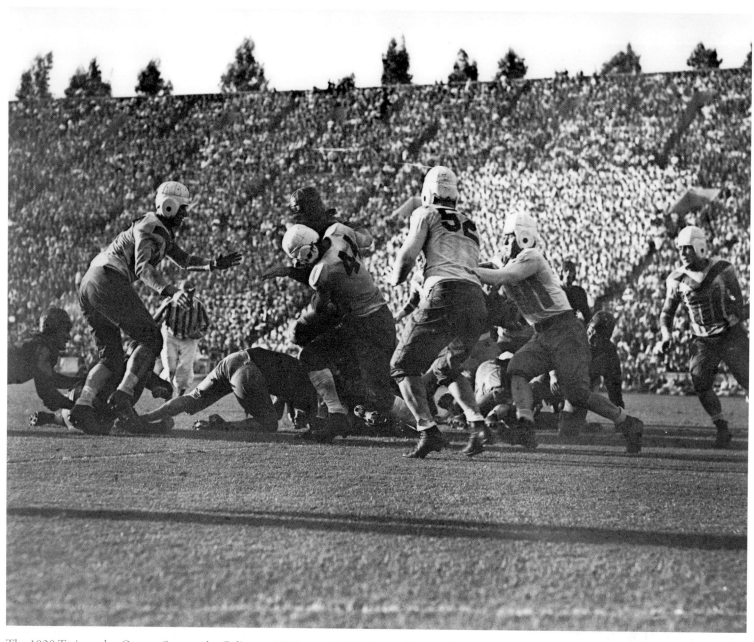

The 1928 Trojans play Oregon State at the Coliseum. USC won 19–0 in front of 50,000. Two other games that season, both at the Coliseum, were far more momentous. The Trojans defeated Stanford 10–0 in front of 80,000, giving Howard Jones his first victory over fellow coach Glenn "Pop" Warner in his fourth try. And USC beat Notre Dame for the first time in the third meeting between the two.

Nate Barragar, fourth from the left, was the center on the USC squad that won a national championship in 1928. Here he is with his 1929 offensive line, captain of a team that concluded its season with a 47–14 victory over Pittsburgh in the 1930 Rose Bowl. Barragar would go on to play pro football with Minneapolis, Frankford, and Green Bay.

Francis Tappaan, shown here in 1929, was an All-American end that year for USC. His biggest catch that season was the one he turned into the only touchdown in a 7–0 win over Stanford. Tappaan also played hockey for USC and went on to a distinguished career as an attorney, judge, legislative analyst, and Department of Justice officer.

USC quarterbacks Russell Saunders (ball in hand) and Marshall Duffield (to his right) follow their blockers in this 1929 shot at practice. Leading the charge are two All-Americans, Johnny Baker (at the left) and Erny Pinckert (third from the left), with Harry Edelson in the middle. Less than a month later, Saunders and Duffield would combine for 279 yards and 4 touchdowns in the Trojans' Rose Bowl victory.

A Coliseum crowd of 79,000 watches USC play Cal in 1929. The visitors would win 15–7, giving Jones his first loss to the Golden Bears. When he arrived, USC had suffered through a nine-game winless streak against Cal. Jones had stopped the agony with two wins and a tie in the preceding three years.

This is a 1930 shot of halfback-end Garrett Arbelbide. He was an All-American that season and a member of the 1931 squad that won USC's second national championship. Arbelbide also played baseball for the Trojans and played one season professionally (1933) with the Hollywood Stars of the Pacific Coast League.

Any thoughts that the Trojans might slide back into their losing ways against Cal, after having been defeated the year before, were shattered in this 1930 game. USC blasted Cal out of the Coliseum 74–0. Somewhere, Gloomy Gus Henderson, who had lost five straight to Cal, had to be cracking a rare smile.

Another shot of the USC domination of Cal in 1930. Trojan assistant coach Gordon Campbell was handling the substitutions in this game. Head coach Howard Jones told Campbell to ease off when the score reached 54–0, but Campbell, according to the book *Traditionally Yours,* ignored the request and continued to pour it on.

USC halfback Erny Pinckert, center, is shown holding the document certifying he is a member of the 1930 All-America team. Shaking Pinckert's hand is Stanford coach Glenn "Pop" Warner. Looking on is Christy Walsh, a newspaperman, author, and member of the All-America Board of Football. Pinckert would make the All-America team again in 1931.

A photo of the 1931 Trojans, the second USC squad to win the national championship. Under Jones, the team lost its opener to St. Mary's 13–7, then went undefeated the rest of the way, finishing 10-1, including 7-0 in conference. The final game was a 21–12 victory over Tulane in the Rose Bowl.

USC coach Howard Jones, on the left, poses with center Stan Williamson, the captain of his 1931 national champions. Williamson, an All-American in 1931, was later an assistant football coach at Kansas State and Oklahoma, and a teacher, coach, and athletic director at UC Santa Barbara.

This is Trojan quarterback Gaius "Gus" Shaver, an All-American who led the 1931 national champs in rushing (936 yards) and scoring (100 points). He came back to USC as an assistant coach from 1940 to 1945 and subsequently became a construction-equipment salesman and a rancher.

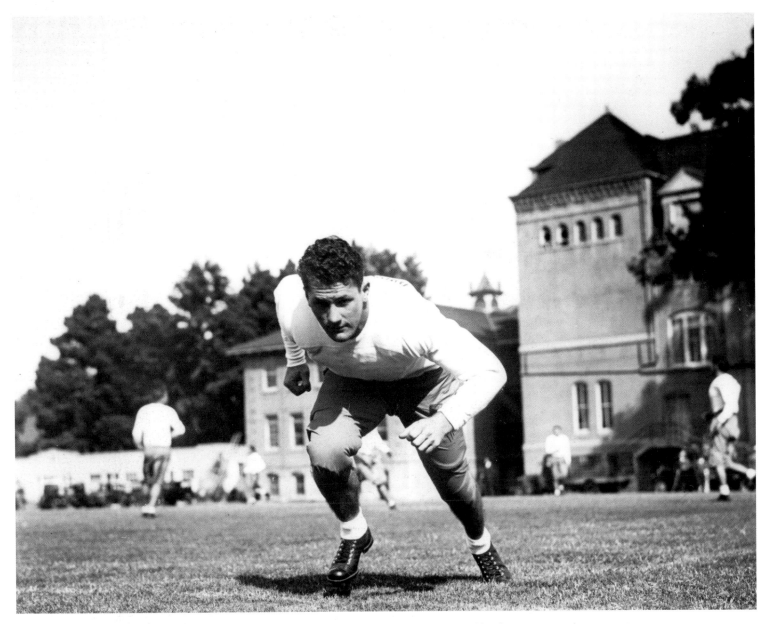

This is Johnny Baker, an All-American guard-kicker for the 1931 Trojans. With one swing of his foot on November 21, 1931, Baker earned a special place in USC history. With one minute to play at Notre Dame, Baker kicked a 33-yard field goal to give the Trojans a 16–14 victory. It was USC's first win at Notre Dame and ended the Fighting Irish's 26-game unbeaten streak.

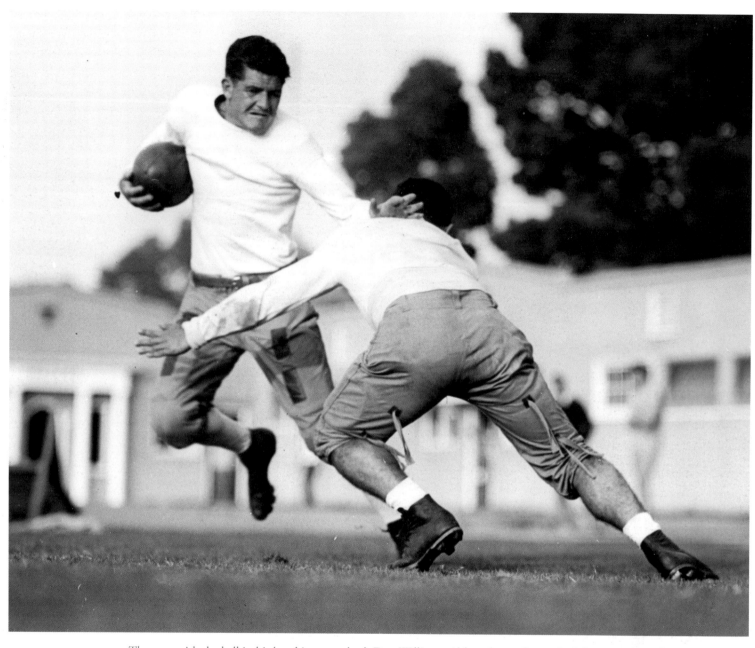

The man with the ball in his hand is quarterback Don Williams. Although standing only 5-foot-9 and weighing 158 pounds, Williams put up some big numbers in 1928. An All-American that season, he rushed for 681 yards and scored 47 points.

USC quarterback Orv Mohler was a 1930 All-American, leading his team in rushing (983 yards) and scoring (102 points) that season. He played on national championship teams for the Trojans in 1931 (the year this photo was taken) and 1932. Mohler later joined the Air Force, became a colonel, and died in the crash of his plane in 1949.

When USC beat the Fighting Irish for the first time at Notre Dame in 1931, the train bringing the team home was dubbed the Victory Special. When it stopped in Chicago, the players donned derby hats as shown here.

The magnitude of USC's last-minute, 16–14 victory over Notre Dame at South Bend can be seen in the size of the newspaper headline being held up by students in this photo. A celebratory parade through downtown Los Angeles drew an estimated 300,000.

These are the 1932 Trojans, winners of the university's second consecutive national championship. Unlike a year earlier when USC lost its season opener and then ran the table, the 1932 team went 10-0. The Trojans finished up with a pair of shutouts, beating Notre Dame 13–0 and Pittsburgh in the Rose Bowl 35–0.

Teammates Ernie Smith (right), Rupert Black (middle), and Al Plaehn (left) perform for the camera in this 1930 photo. Two seasons later, Smith became USC's first unanimous All-American. He was later inducted into the National Football Foundation College Football Hall of Fame and played professionally for Green Bay.

On the receiving end of the snap from center in this 1932 photo is Homer Griffith, a quarterback who played on USC's back-to-back national champion team in 1931-32 and on the 1933 team as well. Griffith was the Player of the Game in the 1933 Rose Bowl, scoring a touchdown in the Trojans' 35–0 victory over Pittsburgh. Griffith played one season in the NFL with the Chicago Cardinals.

Although he's shown catching a pass here in 1932, Raymond "Tay" Brown was a tackle for USC, captain of the 1932 national champion team, an All-American that season, and is a member of the National Football Foundation College Football Hall of Fame. Brown was also a member of the 1931 Trojan track team that won the NCAA title.

Irvine "Cotton" Warburton (shown here in 1933) followed in the footsteps of John Wayne in making the leap from USC to Hollywood. But in Warburton's case, those footsteps left a far greater imprint on Trojan history. USC's leading rusher in 1932 (420 yards) and 1933 (885), Warburton was also USC's leading scorer (72 points) in 1933. He went on to become an Oscar-winning film editor for the classic film *Mary Poppins.*

Aaron Rosenberg, shown here in 1933, was an All-American both that season and the season before. A guard, he was part of a 27-game unbeaten streak, including 25 straight wins, by the Trojans. A member of the National Football Foundation College Football Hall of Fame, Rosenberg was another who moved into the entertainment business after football, becoming a movie and television producer and director.

Stung by having their 27-game unbeaten streak broken by a 13–7 loss to Stanford, the Trojans struck back with three consecutive shutouts toward the end of the 1933 season. The game shown here was the last of those after victories over Oregon (26–0) and Notre Dame (19–0). USC is seen en route to a 31–0 win over Georgia in front of 45,000 at the Coliseum.

The 1934 Trojans are shown going through their final practice before the season opener. It would be a successful start, a 20–0 victory over Occidental. But there would be few such satisfying moments once the competition got stiffer. USC wound up 4-6-1 in 1934, including a dismal 1-4-1 record and a seventh-place finish in the conference.

Trojans hit the tackling dummy in a 1934 practice. They obviously didn't hit the opposition quite so effectively. Howard Jones had lost a total of 11 games in nine previous seasons at USC before losing just over half that many in 1934 alone.

USC guard Bill Radovich (third from left on the offensive line in this 1935 photo) played from 1935 to 1937, then went on to pro football. He spent five years with the Detroit Lions and two seasons with the Los Angeles Dons of the All-America Football Conference. Radovich subsequently sued the NFL, claiming it wouldn't let him return to the league, and eventually settled for $42,500.

Imagine having the guy in black as your fullback, a hulk who could seemingly flick would-be tacklers away like gnats. Actually, the man in the center of this 1935 gag photo with Trojans draped all over him is Ed "Strangler" Lewis, a wrestling star.

The 1937 Trojans are shown facing Washington at the Coliseum in front of 70,000. USC would lose the game 7–0 and go on to end the season 4-4-2, and 2-3-2 in conference. It was the third time in four years that the Trojans, under Jones, failed to finish with a winning record.

This is USC guard Harry Smith in 1938, the first of his two consecutive All-American seasons. A member of the National Football Foundation College Football Hall of Fame, Smith, known as Blackjack, was also on the Trojan rugby team. He played for the Detroit Lions in 1940, and later coached Missouri and the Saskatchewan Roughriders.

Here is USC quarterback Grenville "Grenny" Lansdell at a 1939 practice. Lansdell, who played from 1937 to 1939, was the Trojans' leading passer all three seasons, and the club's leading rusher and scorer in 1938 and 1939. He played one season, 1940, in the NFL with the New York Giants.

USC faces Duke in the 1939 Rose Bowl. The hero of the game was the Trojans' Doyle Nave, a fourth-string quarterback who had previously played only 28 ½ minutes. He came off the bench to complete four straight passes to backup end Al Krueger. The last was a 19-yarder with 40 seconds to play that gave USC a 7–3 victory. Those were the only points Duke surrendered all season.

THE QUIET YEARS

(1941–1959)

Tough record to emulate? Impossible as it turned out. There was no Gloomy Gus, no Headman waiting in the wings when those sideline masters left the stage. But fortunately for the Trojans, there also wasn't much competition for the dollars and support of L.A. sports fans. The Rams were still in Cleveland, the Dodgers were in Brooklyn, the Lakers didn't even exist, and John Wooden was coaching high school basketball as the 1940s began.

It wasn't as if the Trojans were bad over the next two decades. They appeared in six Rose Bowls. They even had an undefeated season in the midst of World War II, going 8-0-2 in 1944, culminating with a 25–0 victory in the Rose Bowl. But the peaks USC had scaled under Elmer Henderson and Howard Jones proved to be unreachable goals for the Trojans of the 1940s and 1950s. There were no national championships, no victories worthy of a parade that could attract 300,000. Yes, there were the six Rose Bowl appearances, but USC walked off that field a winner only three times.

Under Jones, the Trojans produced 20 All-Americans in his 16 seasons. In the ensuing 19 years, there were 11 All-Americans. And perhaps most painful of all, USC's bitter rivalry against Notre Dame, at least competitive under Jones, was disastrous in the 1940s and 1950s. Jones lost his last game against the Fighting Irish in 1940 to drop USC to 6-8-1 against them. Counting that 1940 game, the Trojans were 3-13-1 against Notre Dame over the ensuing two decades, including an embarrassing stretch in which they were 1-10-1.

It certainly wasn't all bleak. There were back-to-back Rose Bowl victories over Washington and Tennessee in 1944 and 1945, the latter completing the unbeaten season. There was the 14–14 tie with Notre Dame in 1948 to end the Fighting Irish's 21-game winning streak. There was a 21–14 victory over top-ranked Cal in 1951 to end the Bears' 38-game, regular-season undefeated streak. There was a 7–0 victory over Wisconsin in the 1953 Rose Bowl. And there were stars like Frank Gifford, John Ferraro, Paul Cleary, Jim Sears, Jon Arnett, Ron Mix, and the McKeever twins, Mike and Marlin. But this era paled in comparison with the excellence of the past and the unseen brilliance that lay just over the horizon.

Washington State running back Felix Fletcher is seen racing for the end zone at the Coliseum with USC defender Bill Bundy (no. 25) in futile pursuit. Fletcher accounted for Washington State's only points on a 12-yard touchdown pass from Billy Sewell in a 7–6 loss to the Trojans in 1941 in front of a crowd of 40,000.

USC coach Jeff Cravath on the sidelines. He took over the reins in 1942 and coached for nine seasons. Cravath played for the Trojans for three seasons (1924–26). As the team's coach, he was 54-28-8 and took USC to four Rose Bowls, winning two of them. After finishing 2-5-2 in 1950, Cravath was fired.

Although the opponent in this 1942 game is unknown, the emotions displayed here are quite clear. As Jeff Cravath, in his first season as USC head coach, embraces one of his players on the sideline, the other Trojans are obviously also enjoying what has occurred on the field.

USC tackle John Ferraro (right) poses in 1944 with his coach, Jeff Cravath. The 6-foot-4, 240-pound Ferraro was an All-American in 1944 and 1947. He played for the Trojans from 1943 to 1947, with the exception of 1945, a year in which he served in the military. A member of the National Football Foundation College Football Hall of Fame, Ferraro later became a Los Angeles city councilman.

USC plays Tennessee in the 1945 Rose Bowl. In front of a capacity crowd of 91,000, the Trojans, behind quarterback Jim Hardy, won 25–0. Hardy threw two touchdown passes and scored a third himself. With the nation at war, Tennessee put a largely freshman team on the field.

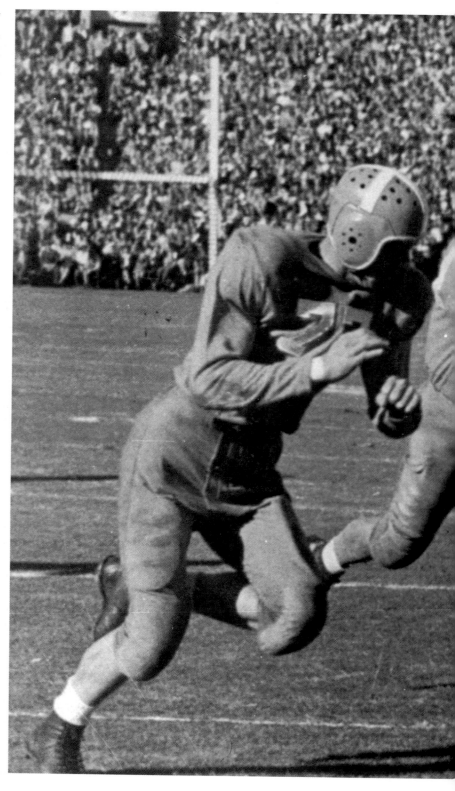

USC receiver Harry Adelman catches a touchdown pass in the end zone in the fourth quarter of the 1946 Rose Bowl despite the tight coverage of Alabama defender Hugh Morrow. Unfortunately for the Trojans, they were behind 34–0 when Verl Lillywhite connected with Adelman from 25 yards out and would go on to lose 34–14. It was USC's first defeat in the New Year's Day game after eight victories.

USC battles Rice in 1947. The Trojans trailed 7–0 with just over two minutes remaining in a game played in the Coliseum in front of 64,231. Rice was still looking for its next points against the Trojans when USC tied the game with 2:10 to play, and that's the way it ended. In two subsequent meetings, the Trojans beat Rice 7–0 (1948) and 24–0 (1971).

In this 1948 game, played at night in the Coliseum in front of 55,211 fans, USC beat Utah 27–0, making the cumulative score between the two teams 169–9 over a five-game span beginning in 1917. They have played only twice since 1948, USC winning again in 1993 before Utah finally broke into the win column in 2001.

A Coliseum crowd of 100,571 watches USC and Notre Dame in 1948. The Fighting Irish came in with a 21-game winning streak and were facing a Trojan squad that had lost three times in nine games. But Notre Dame had to settle for a 14–14 tie. And to get that, the Irish scored on a touchdown run by Emil Sitko from a yard out and got the extra point with 35 seconds remaining in the game.

The Trojans are shown suffering through their worst defeat ever in a Rose Bowl game, a 49–0 loss to Michigan in 1948. Forty-six years earlier, Michigan had faced Stanford in the first bowl game ever, played at Tournament Park in Pasadena. Final score: Michigan 49, Stanford 0.

On the left is halfback-safety Jim Sears in 1952, the year he made the All-American team. That season, the last of his three as a Trojan, Sears led the team in total offense, scoring, completions, passing yards, and punt-return yardage. As a pro, he played for the Chicago Cardinals in the NFL and the Los Angeles Chargers and Denver Broncos in the AFL.

The man in the black suit and fedora is Jess Hill, who succeeded Jeff Cravath as USC head coach and lasted six seasons (1951-56). Hill compiled an impressive 45-17-1 record, but led the Trojans to only two Rose Bowl appearances and a single victory, over Wisconsin in 1953. He took USC back to Pasadena in 1955, but the Trojans lost to Ohio State.

He is remembered for his 12 seasons with the New York Giants, for the 1958 NFL championship game against the Baltimore Colts, and for his years as a sports announcer, particularly on TV's Monday Night Football. But before all that, Frank Gifford was a Trojan (1949-51). And a good one on offense, defense, and as a kicker. He is shown here in 1951, his All-American season.

Following Spread: The Trojan Marching Band sometime in the 1950s. This band is older than the team, having begun in 1880, the year the university was founded. Over the years, the band has gained worldwide fame in marches around the globe, appearing everywhere from the Great Wall of China to the remnants of the Berlin Wall to France for the 50th anniversary of the D-Day landing.

This is USC against Wisconsin in the 1953 Rose Bowl, played in front of 101,500. The Trojans won 7–0, giving the Pacific Coast Conference its first victory over the Big Ten since the signing of the 1946 agreement by the two conferences to meet in the Rose Bowl. Winning coach Jess Hill became first to have both played for (1929) and coached a Rose Bowl winner.

Al Carmichael (no. 21, at left) heads up the field in the 1953 Rose Bowl. Carmichael caught a 22-yard touchdown pass from Rudy Bukich, the culmination of a 73-yard, third-quarter drive, for the only points of the game in a 7–0 USC victory over Wisconsin.

This is "Jaguar" Jon Arnett in 1955. An All-American that season, Arnett played for the Trojans from 1954 to 1956. A member of the National Football Foundation College Football Hall of Fame, Arnett was not only an offensive and defensive star, but a team-leading kick returner as well. As a pro, he played for the Los Angeles Rams and the Chicago Bears.

A Coliseum end zone shot of USC and UCLA in 1958. With 58,507 looking on, the Bruins' John Brown intercepted a lateral and raced 45 yards to the end zone to give UCLA a 15–7 fourth-quarter lead. Not for long. The Trojans' Luther Hayes ran back the ensuing kickoff 74 yards for a touchdown of his own. USC added a two-point conversion and the game ended 15–15.

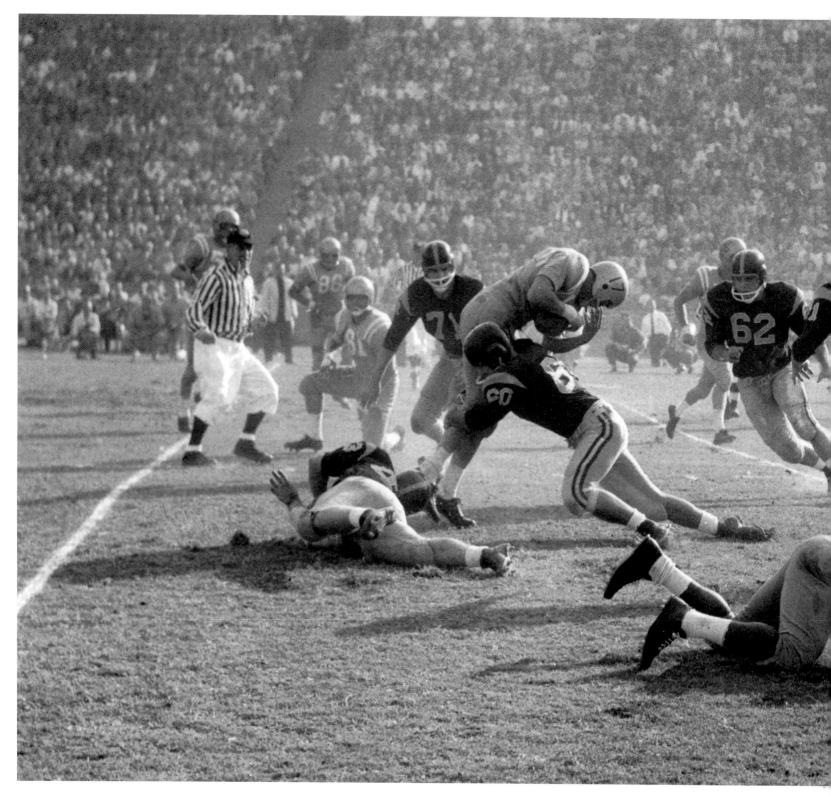

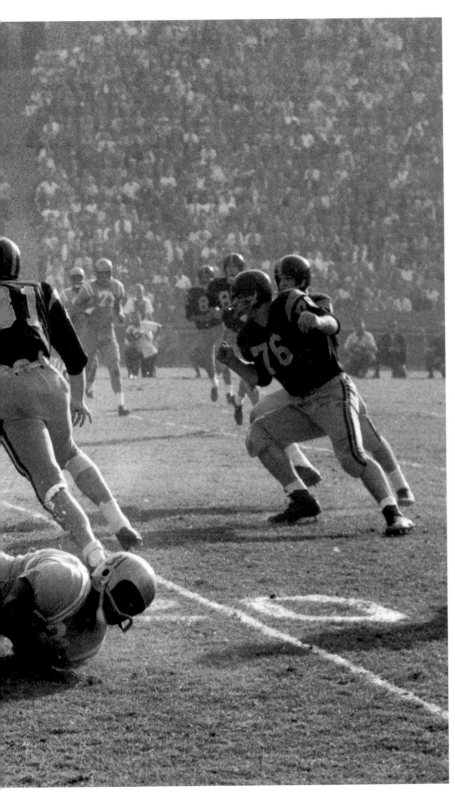

USC is shown again playing its crosstown rivals, the UCLA Bruins. With the two schools sharing the same city, the same stadium, and battling for the same recruits, this was often the biggest game of the year for both schools. Not in the beginning, however. The Trojans won the first two games (1929-30) 76–0 and 52–0, and the two universities didn't play again for six years.

USC head coach Don Clark poses with his staff in 1959, his third season at the helm. The key figure in this shot, however, is the man second from the right, first-year assistant John McKay. One year later, McKay would replace Clark and launch a new era of Trojan excellence.

Looming behind the twin blocking dummies are the McKeever twins, Marlin and Mike. Not only were they twin brothers, they were twins in their love of football and in their skills as well. Both made All-American in 1959 for USC. Marlin was a repeat honoree in 1960. Mike would die at 27 after 22 months in a coma as a result of an automobile accident.

Living in the same town as the Bruins after a loss is tough for the Trojans. This 1959 game between the two was the end of a tough decade for USC. UCLA won 10–3, handing the Trojans two losses and a tie in their last three games against UCLA and an overall 2-7-1 mark for USC in the rivalry in the 1950s.

THE GLORY YEARS

(1960–1980)

If thunder was the apt word to describe the USC Trojan herd that rumbled across college football in the 1920s and 1930s, crushing defenses in their path, then lightning might best describe the teams of the 1960s and 1970s.

Under the direction of coaches John McKay and John Robinson, behind imposing offensive lines, utilizing the effectiveness of the I-formation, a generation of USC tailbacks led the school back to glory with lightning-quick moves, blinding speed, and zig-zagging paths to the end zone. Three of those Trojans ran not only to daylight, but to the top of the list for the Heisman Trophy in votes. There was Mike Garrett, only 5-foot-9 and 185 pounds, but fast, elusive, and strong enough to shake off would-be tacklers and to serve as an effective blocker. There was O. J. Simpson, whose brilliance as one of the greatest runners in college football history has certainly been dimmed by the double-murder charges against him in the 1990s, but he will never be forgotten by those who saw him in action. In the 1967 showdown with UCLA alone, Simpson completed two of the most memorable scoring runs ever. And there was Charles White, whose ability in the open field was sometimes overshadowed by his bruising style inside. Two other Trojan running backs from that era—Anthony Davis and Ricky Bell—were runners-up for the Heisman.

It all began with McKay, a former Oregon assistant who became USC's coach in 1960. After two dismal seasons (4-6, 4-5-1), along came 1962, the start of a period that would have made Howard Jones proud. McKay's Trojans were 11-0 that season and winners of a national championship. It was the beginning of a 14-season run in which McKay's teams won four national championships and appeared in eight Rose Bowls, winning five of them. When McKay left after the 1975 season to coach an NFL expansion team, the Tampa Bay Buccaneers, an unheralded former USC assistant named John Robinson took over seamlessly, going 11-1 and winning the Rose Bowl in his first season. By his third year, he had his first national championship and another Rose Bowl victory.

As the Trojans headed into their tenth decade, yet another generation was proving worthy of maintaining the standard of excellence established so long before.

This is Traveler, USC's mascot, with rider Richard Saukko astride in the 1960s. After Saukko was spotted riding his white horse in the 1961 Rose Parade, he was asked to saddle up for Trojan games. He did so until ill health forced him out of the saddle in 1988. The tradition has continued with other riders and six Travelers over the years, following in the hoofprints of the original.

This 1960 photo shows new Trojan head coach John McKay, at right, conducting a chalk talk with his staff. Over the ensuing 16 seasons, McKay would become the winningest coach in USC history with 127 victories. Along with McKay's impressive record (127-40-8) would come an even more impressive number: 4. That's how many national championships his Trojans would win.

USC receiver Hal Bedsole tries to conduct a chalk talk of his own, but actress Rhonda Fleming isn't paying attention in this 1962 publicity shot. Bedsole was an All-American that season, leading a team bound for the national championship in catches (33) and scoring (68 points). Against Cal that season, Bedsole had chalked up a then-team record 201 receiving yards.

Coach John McKay, left, confers with assistant coach Marv Goux, right, and receiver Rod Sherman in this photo from the 1960s. Sherman (1964-66) is best known for catching a 15-yard touchdown pass from Craig Fertig with 1:33 to play to upset undefeated and top-ranked Notre Dame 20–17 in 1964. Goux was a Trojan assistant for 26 seasons (1957-82).

Coach John McKay congratulates fullback Ben Wilson after he scored a touchdown in the Trojans' 25–0 shellacking of Notre Dame at the Coliseum in front of 81,676. Wilson scored twice in the first half to give USC the momentum to wrap up an undefeated regular season and a Rose Bowl berth.

USC linebacker Damon Bame secures the ball carrier in a 1962 game at the Coliseum between the Trojans and Navy in front of 51,701. In an undefeated season that would lead to a national championship, this was one of USC's tougher games, the Trojans winning 13–6.

UCLA punter Tom Bennett gets the ball off just beyond the grasp of onrushing Trojan John Brownwood (no. 88) in this photo from the 1963 game between the two schools. USC won 26–6 in front of a Coliseum crowd of 82,460. With Mike Garrett contributing 119 rushing yards, the Trojans piled up 530 yards in total offense to only 314 yards for the Bruins.

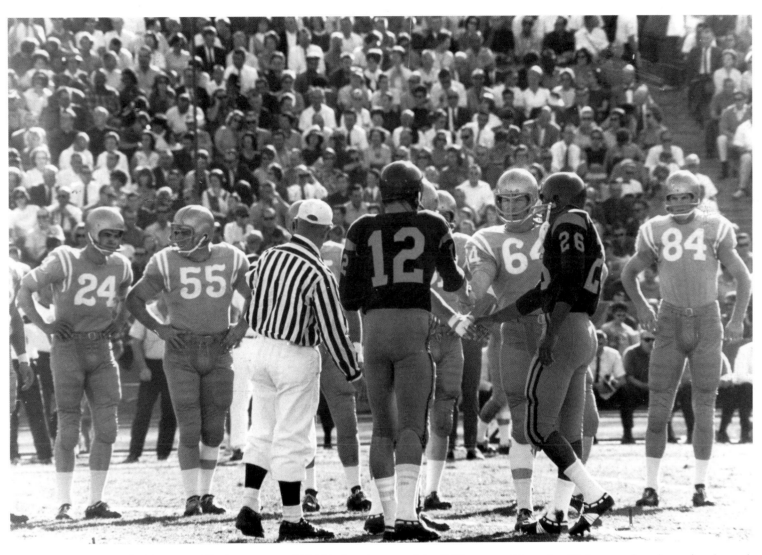

The Trojans and Bruins meet at midfield before the start of the 1963 game on November 30. It was to have been played a week earlier on November 23, but was canceled following the assassination of President John F. Kennedy the day before in Dallas.

USC tailback Willie Brown tries to elude a Wisconsin defender in the 1963 Rose Bowl. It was one of the wildest Rose Bowls
ever with the Trojans hanging on for a 42–37 win in a game in which 11 Rose Bowl records were broken. USC led 42–14 until
Wisconsin quarterback Ron Vander Kelen led a furious Badger rally.

The USC varsity at a Trojan rally in 1964. Ultimately, there wasn't much to cheer about by season's end. Although the team finished 7-3 and tied for the conference title with a 3-1 record, Oregon State, with an 8-3 overall record, was given the Rose Bowl berth.

This is Mike Garrett in 1964, a key figure in USC history, both on and off the field. He was the first of the Trojan tailbacks to run to Heisman glory, winning college football's most coveted trophy in 1965. After playing for both the Kansas City Chiefs and the San Diego Chargers, and appearing in two Super Bowls, he came back to USC and was named athletic director in 1993.

USC kicks off in a 1964 game. This was the middle of a frustrating period for the Trojans. After winning a national championship in 1962, they went through three seasons with impressive records (7-3, 7-3, 7-2-1) and some big wins, but not even a Rose Bowl berth to show for it.

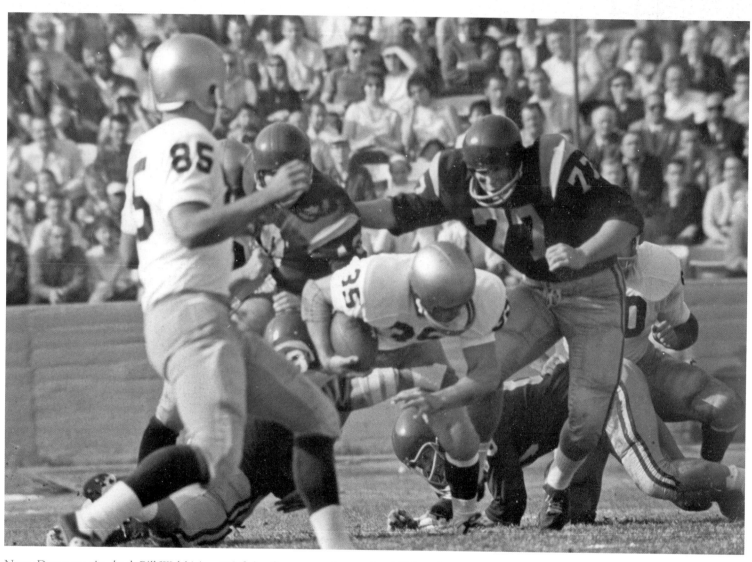

Notre Dame running back Bill Wolski (no. 35) fights for extra yardage against USC in their 1964 game at the Coliseum in front of 83,840. Notre Dame, entering the game with a 9-0 record to face the 6-3 Trojans, was battling for a national championship. USC took the fight out of the Fighting Irish, winning 20–17.

Having lost the 1963 Rose Bowl to the Trojans, Wisconsin wanted a rematch. The Badgers got it on their home field in 1965, but it wasn't worth the wait. USC won 26–6 in front of 52,706. The frustration can be seen here as Wisconsin running back Vernon Hackbart is surrounded by Trojans.

USC plays Oregon State in a 1965 night game at the Coliseum before a crowd of 52,100. USC won 26–12. It was the second victory in a row for the Trojans over the Beavers, but just the beginning of a decades-long period of domination. Over a span of 37 years beginning in 1963, USC would go 29-1 against Oregon State, including 26 wins in a row.

Hopes were high among the Trojans when this 1965 photo was taken. They were on their way to a 14–0 victory over Stanford at the Coliseum in front of 61,618. Expectations would dim as the season wore on. The victory gave USC a 4-0-1 record, but subsequent losses to Notre Dame and UCLA would kill any hope of a return to the top of the rankings or to Pasadena.

USC and Stanford get into a sideline-clearing scuffle in their 1965 game at the Coliseum. While Notre Dame and UCLA are generally considered the Trojans' bitterest rivals, the relationship between USC and Stanford has often been heated as well. John McKay, the Trojans' coach in 1965, once referred to people from Stanford as "those snooty bastards," according to the book *Fight On*.

USC defensive end and kicker Tim Rossovich, a 1967 All-American, is shown in 1965 kicking one of eight extra points, then a school record, against Wyoming in a 56–6 Trojan victory at the Coliseum. Rossovich played in the NFL with the Philadelphia Eagles, San Diego Chargers, and Houston Oilers, and was later an actor and stuntman.

USC fullback Dan Scott (no. 38) leads the blocking for Steve Grady (no. 21) in this 1966 night game at the Coliseum against Wisconsin in front of 52,325 fans. The Trojans won 38–3, giving the university its 400th football victory.

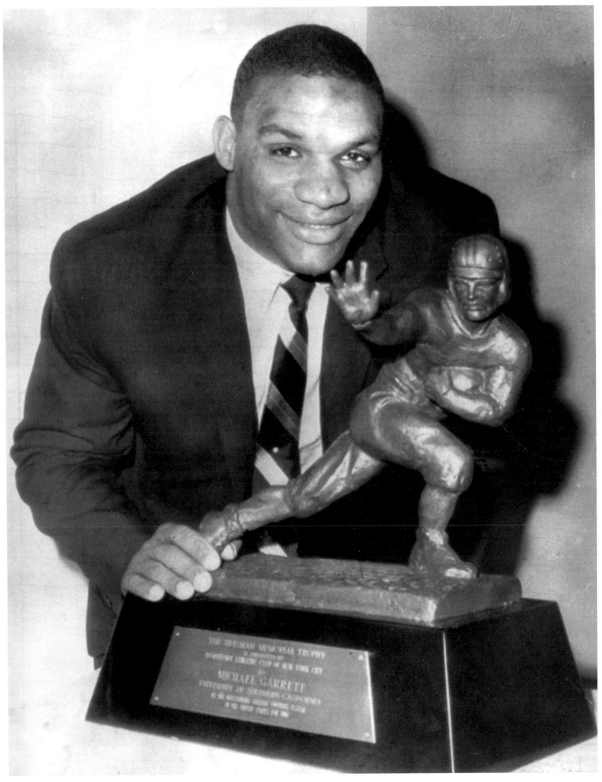

Trojan tailback Mike Garrett poses with his Heisman Trophy in 1965. That was the culmination of his three seasons at USC in which he set a then-NCAA record with 3,221 career rushing yards. Garrett was the first player to lead both the Trojans and the conference in rushing three straight years, including an NCAA-leading 1,440 yards in 1965.

With assistant coach Marv Goux looking on, the Trojans go through drills in spring practice, 1967. In this case, practice didn't make perfect, but pretty close. USC went on that season to a 10-1 record, a national championship, and a victory over Indiana in the Rose Bowl.

USC tailback O. J. Simpson goes airborne in 1967. His legacy will be forever soiled by murder charges and incarceration in his later years, but back in his playing days, Simpson was a football hero, winner of the 1968 Heisman Trophy, and a 2,000-yard, single-season rusher with the Buffalo Bills in the NFL.

Once again, Trojan fullback Dan Scott (no. 38) runs interference, this time for halfback Jim Lawrence in a 1967 game played at Cal. The top-ranked Trojans won 31–12 to improve their spotless record to 8-0. It was also USC's ninth straight win over Cal in a streak that would end at 11.

USC defensive tackle Tony Terry tries to bring down Miami's John Acuff in this 1968 game at the Coliseum, attended by 71,189. The Trojans won 28–3 and would be unbeaten until the Rose Bowl where, as the number 2–ranked team in the nation, they would lose to top-ranked Ohio State 27–16.

The figure at center, USC coach John McKay, is caught in a familiar pose from the 1968-69 seasons, hands behind his back, head down as he paces. It wasn't easy being coach of the Cardiac Kids as those two teams were known. Twelve times they won or tied games with fourth-quarter comebacks including this one, a 20–13 victory at Oregon, in which they scored the winning touchdown with 1:12 to play.

O. J. and his Heisman. Trojan tailback O. J. Simpson won college football's biggest individual trophy in 1968 with the highest point total (2,853) and largest margin of victory (1,750) in Heisman history. In just two seasons at USC (1967-68), he equaled or bettered 19 NCAA, conference, and school records.

USC has had many assistant coaches who have gone on to the NFL: Al Davis, Don Coryell, Steve Mariucci, Norv Turner, and Dave Wannstedt. One of the most successful was Joe Gibbs (at right), who spent 1969 and 1970 on the Trojan sideline. As head coach of the Washington Redskins, Gibbs took his team to four Super Bowls and won three of them.

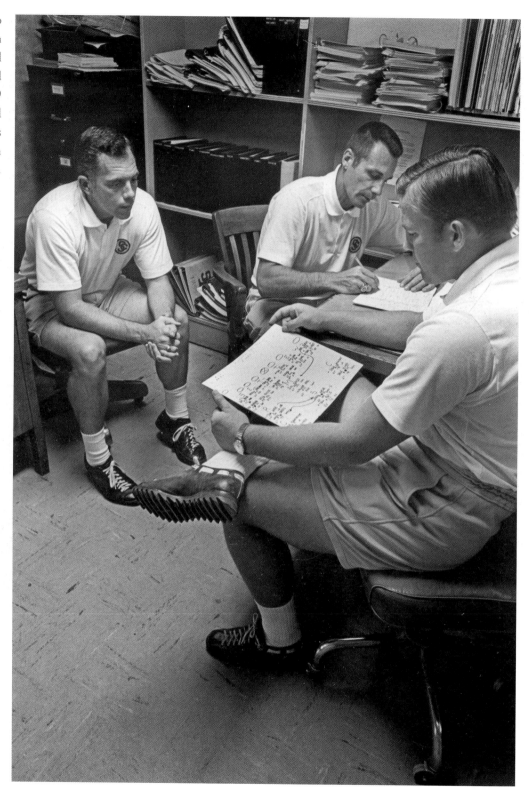

USC defensive tackle Al Cowlings in 1969, his All-American season. After that year, his second with the Trojans, the 6-foot-5, 245-pounder went to the NFL where, at first, he was reunited with teammate O. J. Simpson on the Buffalo Bills. Cowlings also played for the Houston Oilers, Los Angeles Rams, Seattle Seahawks, and San Francisco 49ers.

Jim Fassel cocks his arm in practice in 1969, the season he was on the USC roster as a backup quarterback behind Jimmy Jones. Fassel had far more success wearing headphones than wearing a helmet. He coached in both college and at the pro level, the peak being his seven years with the New York Giants, including one Super Bowl appearance where his team lost to the Baltimore Ravens.

The Wild Bunch poses in 1969. Named after the Sam Peckinpah Western popular at that time, this wild bunch was USC's defensive line, carrying their firepower in their arms and legs. From left to right, tackle Al Cowlings, end Jimmy Gunn, middle guard Willard "Bubba" Scott, end Charlie Weaver, and tackle Tody Smith. The sixth man in the group, not present in this photo, was middle guard Tony Terry.

USC tailback Clarence Davis in 1969, his All-American season. Davis led the Trojans in rushing in both his seasons in cardinal and gold (a conference-leading 1,351 yards in 1969 and 972 yards in 1970). Davis was also the conference kickoff-return leader in 1970 with 444 yards. In the NFL, he played with the Oakland Raiders, appearing in one Super Bowl.

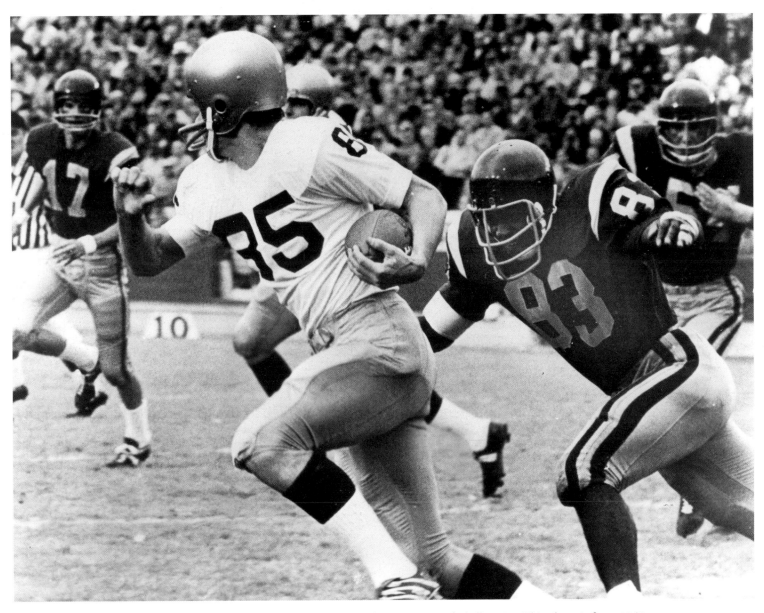

Number 83 is USC defensive tackle Jimmy Gunn in his usual position, hot in pursuit of a ball carrier. This photo is from 1969, his All-American season. Gunn, a member of USC's Wild Bunch, was a Trojan for three seasons and played in three Rose Bowls. In the NFL, he played for the Chicago Bears, New York Giants, and Tampa Bay Buccaneers.

Members of the 1970 USC offensive line (no. 61, guard Allan Graf; no. 60, guard Wayne Yary; and no. 78, offensive tackle Marv Montgomery) go through drills in this photo from a 1970 practice. After producing 1,000-yard rushers for three straight seasons and four of the previous five, the Trojan offense would come up short in 1970. Leading rusher Clarence Davis was stopped at 972 yards.

USC coach John McKay at a 1970 practice. After four straight seasons that ended at the Rose Bowl, including one that also produced a national championship, this season would mark a disappointing drop into mediocrity. The Trojans would finish 6-4-1, but just 3-4 in the conference, plunging USC into a tie for sixth.

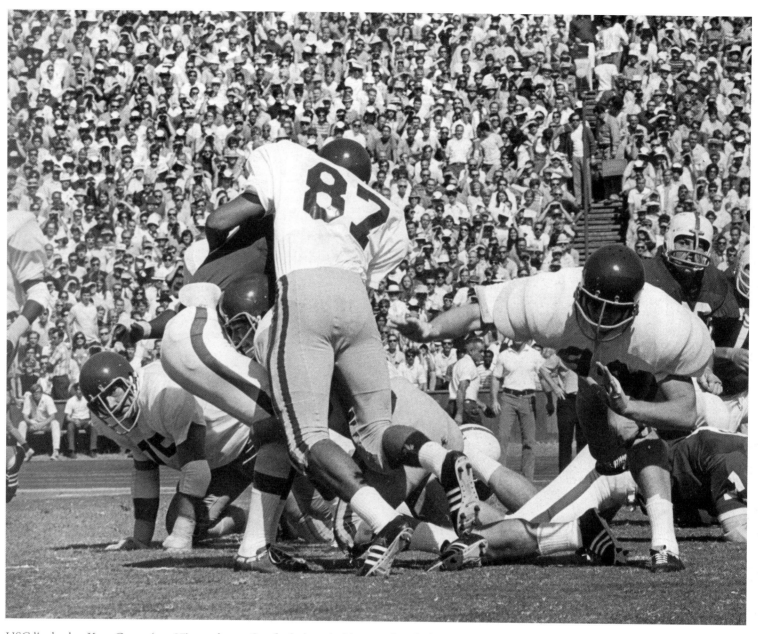

USC linebacker Kent Carter (no. 87) may have a Stanford player in his grasp, but the Trojans couldn't get control of this 1970 game, played at Stanford in front of a capacity crowd of 86,000. The 12th-ranked Indians (Stanford's nickname at the time) beat fourth-ranked USC 24–14, ending a 12-game Trojan winning streak against the Indians.

Even in a bad Trojan year, solace can be found in a victory over Notre Dame. Especially one like this 1970 game. USC came into the Coliseum on a rainy day with a 5-4-1 record and coming off a 45–20 loss to UCLA to face fourth-ranked Notre Dame. In the end, however, it was USC celebrating after a 38–28 win in front of 64,694.

The Rose Bowl on New Year's Day, 1970. It was a good day for fifth-ranked USC, a 10–3 winner over seventh-ranked Michigan. The difference was a 13-yard touchdown pass from Jimmy Jones to Bob Chandler. The Wolverines' despair extended beyond the playing field to coach Bo Schembechler, who missed the game after suffering a heart attack.

A 1972 photo of the USC marching band. The band began appearing at every Trojan road game, in addition to the home games, in 1987 and has not missed a game since. Consisting of 300 members, the band makes 350 appearances a year.

USC Song Girls in 1972, five years after the group was formed with seven members. Things have changed a bit since this photo was taken. Today, the 12-member Song Girl squad dresses in white with cardinal and gold trim, features three dozen new dance routines a year, and performs at various university functions, on the international stage and on both TV and radio.

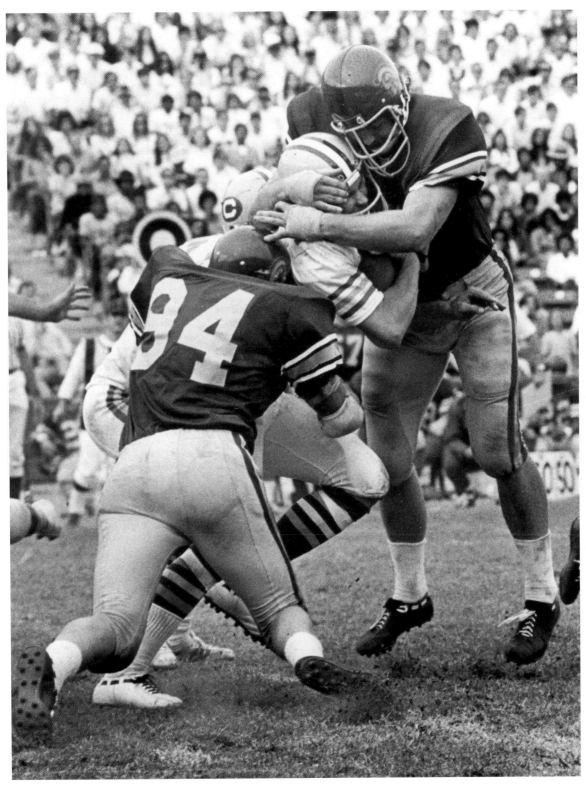

USC defensive lineman John Grant (no. 94) helps halt a Cal player in this 1972 game at the Coliseum. Grant, a Trojan for three seasons, was an All-American in 1972. In the NFL, he played for the Denver Broncos and appeared in one Super Bowl.

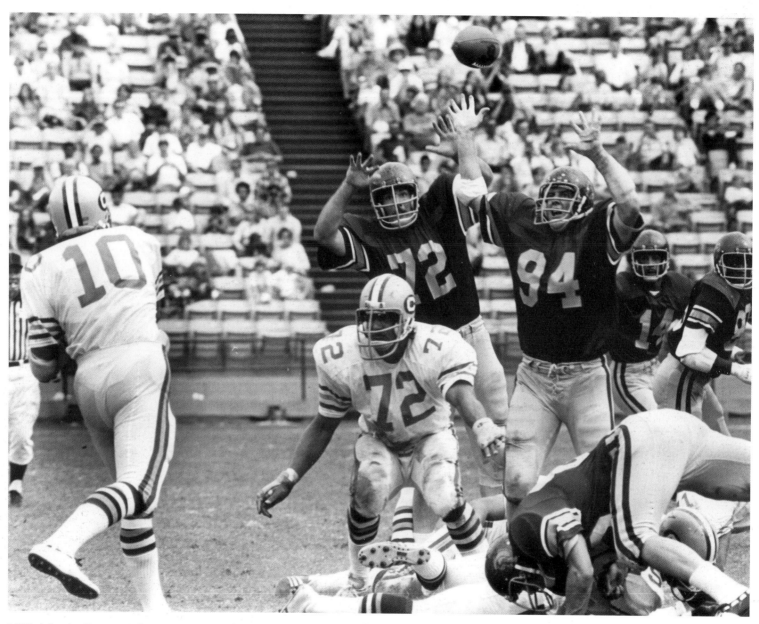

USC defensive lineman John Grant (no. 94) throws up his hands, as does teammate Monte Doris, in an attempt to block a pass by Cal's Steve Bartkowski in this 1972 game. Playing at the Coliseum in front of 56,488, the Trojans, en route to an unbeaten season and a national championship, won 42–14.

USC cheerleaders are adorned with wreaths in this 1972 game. The squad also entertains at Trojan basketball and volleyball games. *Sports Illustrated* named the USC Song Girls the Best Cheerleaders in America. There is also a Trojan Junior Song Girl Camp.

Trojan defenders George Follett (no. 70), Jeff Winans (no. 92), and Dale Mitchell (no. 85) surround a Notre Dame ball carrier in the 1972 clash between the two teams at the Coliseum in front of 75,243. Both defenses struggled as the two teams combined for 68 points, USC winning 45–23.

When the 1972 USC–Notre Dame game ended, this banner told the story. The Trojans, ranked number 1 since the second game of the season, proved they deserved the top spot, finishing the regular season 11-0. And they went on to add one more victory, beating Ohio State 42–17 in the Rose Bowl.

He wasn't as imposing as Traveler, but a lot easier to lift. Although the familiar white horse is the Trojan mascot, a white dog, Turd, became the unofficial mascot of the 1972 squad. Here he is held aloft by his owner, offensive tackle Pete Adams, as coach John McKay addresses the crowd after USC beat Notre Dame. Adams was on the All-American team that season. Turd didn't make the squad.

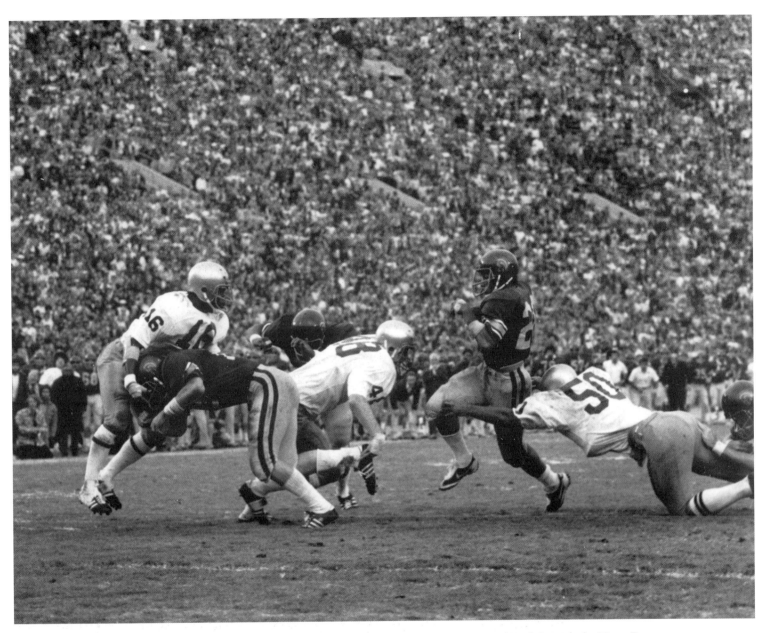

USC tailback Anthony Davis is shown doing what he is best remembered for, running over, around, and through the Notre Dame defense. In his three seasons as a Trojan, Davis scored 44 touchdowns. Eleven of those were against the Irish, including six in the 1972 game and four in 1974. Three of those 11 touchdowns were on kickoff returns (97 and 96 yards in 1972, and 102 yards in 1974).

Anthony Davis (no. 28) celebrates a Trojan moment with quarterback Pat Haden (no. 10) and defensive back Marvin Cobb (no. 24), his teammates from 1972-74. An All-American in 1974, Davis was also an outfielder on USC's national-champion baseball teams of 1973 and 1974. Professionally, Davis played in the NFL, World Football League, and Canadian Football League.

The picture of Lynn Swann that most often comes to mind is of his acrobatic Super Bowl catch as a Pittsburgh Steeler. But this 1973 photo is a reminder that Swann was also a star in college at USC. He was an All-American receiver in 1973 and played in two Rose Bowls before going on to play in four Super Bowls.

With the national championship in their grasp on New Year's Day 1973 (as is Ohio State quarterback Greg Hare in this photo), the Trojans weren't about to let go when they faced the Buckeyes in the Rose Bowl. With Anthony Davis rushing for 157 yards and Mike Rae throwing for 229, USC won 42–17 in front of 106,869, the largest Rose Bowl crowd in history.

Trojan running back Sam "Bam" Cunningham goes over the top to score one of his four touchdowns in the 1973 Rose Bowl against Ohio State. Cunningham shares with several others the Rose Bowl record for most trips to the end zone.

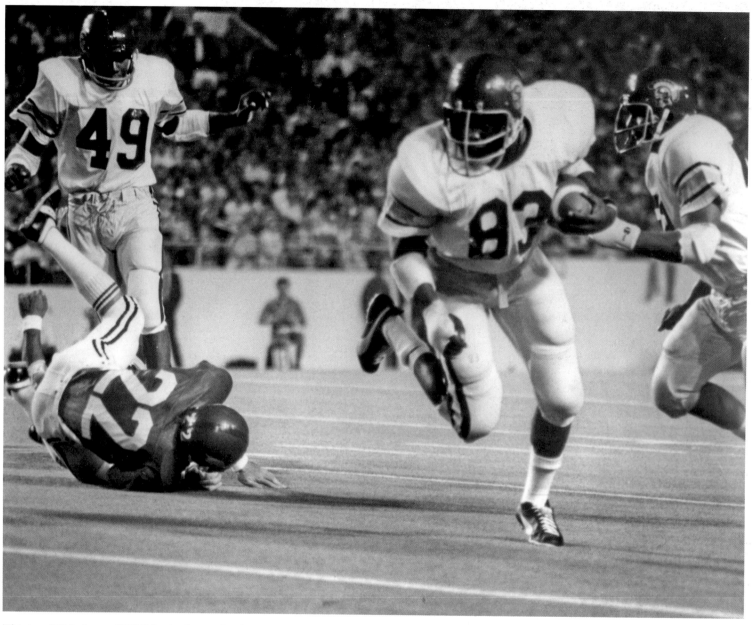

This is a 1974 photo of USC linebacker Richard Wood, better known for hanging onto an opposing player than a football. He was USC's first three-time All-American (1972-74), a consensus choice the last two seasons. Nicknamed Batman, he played in the NFL for the New York Jets and Tampa Bay Buccaneers.

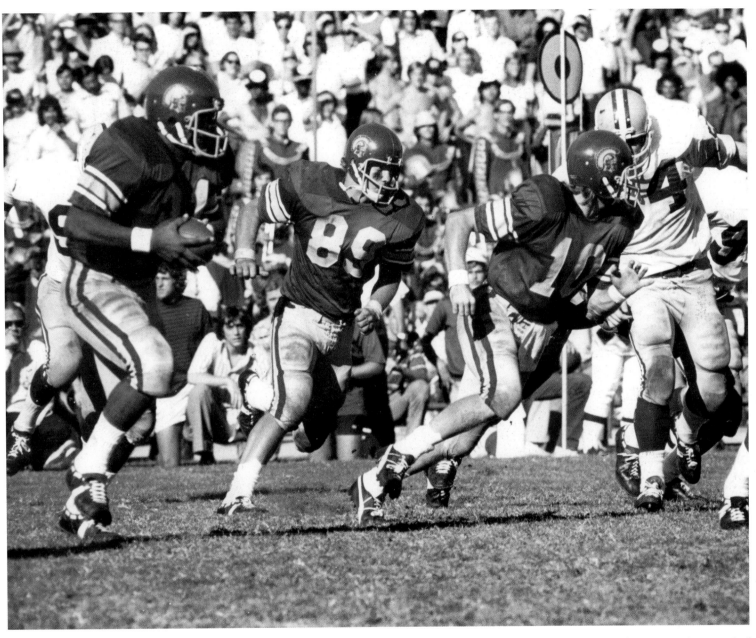

The player in the center of this 1974 photo, tight end Jim Obradovich (no. 89), was an All-American that season, the second of his two years as a Trojan. His brother Steve was a wide receiver for USC two seasons later. Jim played in the NFL for the New York Giants, San Francisco 49ers, and Tampa Bay Buccaneers.

A photo of the USC marching band in 1975. The band has played on the world stage in various countries, and on the national stage in front of various American presidents, including an appearance in conjunction with the 1984 inauguration of Ronald Reagan. But the band is also a familiar sight locally beyond the Coliseum at events like the annual 4th of July parade on Santa Catalina Island.

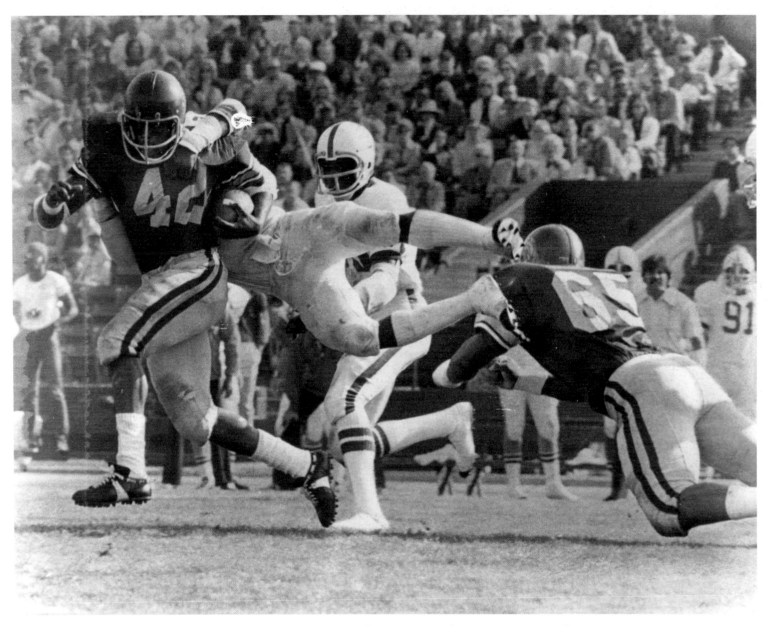

Ricky Bell (no. 42) was another in the long line of spectacular USC tailbacks. A Trojan from 1973 to 1976, Bell was a unanimous All-American in 1975 and 1976. He played in three Rose Bowls and a Liberty Bowl. Bell finished second in voting for the Heisman Trophy in 1976, and third in 1975. He later played for John McKay's Tampa Bay Buccaneers and also played for the San Diego Chargers.

USC defensive tackle Gary Jeter (no. 79) bears down on Purdue quarterback Craig Nagel in this photo from their 1975 game at the Coliseum. USC won 19–6 in front of 56,170. Jeter, who played for the Trojans for four seasons (1973-76), was an All-American in 1976.

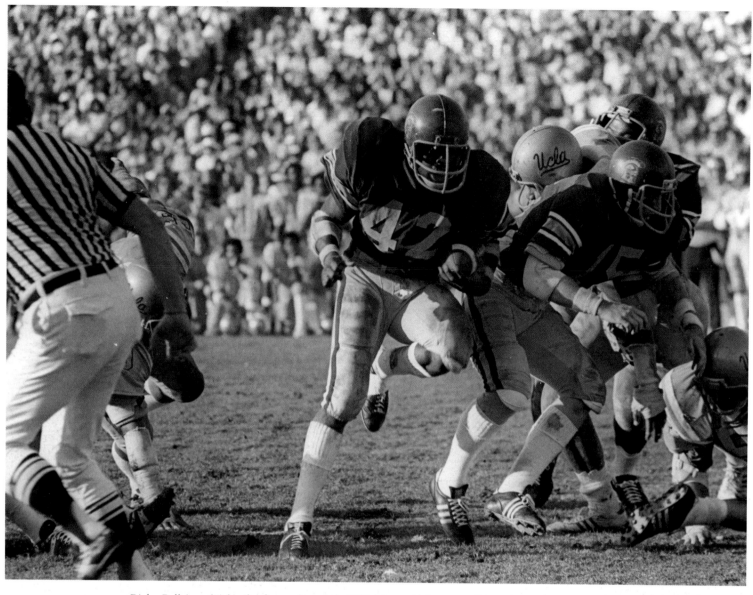

Ricky Bell (no. 42) battles for yards against UCLA in a 1976 game at the Coliseum played in front of 90,519. Despite being hampered by an injured ankle, Bell rushed for 167 yards. At game's end, it was the Bruins who felt the pain, losing 24–14 even though they had come into the game ranked second in the nation with the Trojans at number 3.

USC linebacker Clay Matthews (second from the left) in 1977, his All-American season. Matthews was gone after four years (1974-77), but the Matthews name would keep reappearing on the Trojan roster over the next three decades. His brother, Bruce, was an All-American guard in the 1980s, son Kyle a safety in 2003, and son Clay Matthews III a defensive lineman at USC and Pro Bowler with the Green Bay Packers.

Following Spread: The 1977 Rose Bowl, where third-ranked USC beat second-ranked Michigan 14–6 in front of 106,182. After losing their opening game that season to Missouri, the Trojans ran the table, their victory over the Wolverines giving them an 11-1 record. USC quarterback Vince Evans (with a one-yard run) and tailback Charles White (a seven-yard run) did the scoring and the Trojan defense did the rest.

USC plays Michigan State in a 1978 night game at the Coliseum in front of 65,319. Coming off a victory over top-ranked Alabama, the third-ranked Trojans beat Michigan State 30–9 to run their record to 4–0. But a week later, they stumbled, falling to Arizona State 20–7. That was USC's only loss in a 12-1 season.

USC tailback Charles White in 1978. A Trojan from 1976 to 1979, White was a unanimous All-American in 1978 and 1979 and topped off his college career by winning the 1979 Heisman Trophy, the third Trojan so honored. In the 1980 Rose Bowl, White's third, he set the all-time Rose Bowl rushing record, gaining 247 yards.

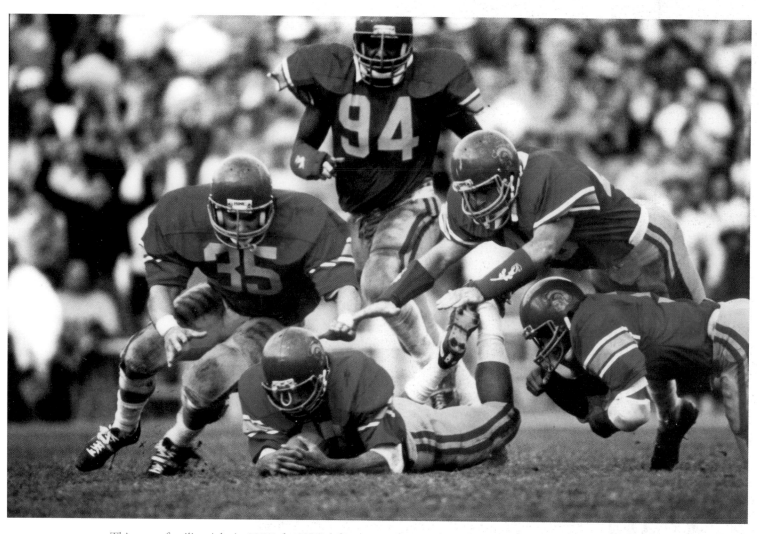

This was a familiar sight in 1978, the USC defense pouncing on a loose ball. With the Trojans winning a national championship that season, the spotlight was on the offense led by two All-Americans (tailback Charles White and offensive tackle Pat Howell) and quarterback Paul McDonald. But an unsung defense allowed only one team, Notre Dame, to score more than 20 points and USC won that game 27–25.

The 1979 Rose Bowl, the climax of another USC national championship. The Trojans, third-ranked coming into the game, beat number 5 Michigan 17–10. USC finished on top of the coaches' poll, but was second in the writers' poll to Alabama, even though the Trojans (12-1) had beaten the Crimson Tide (11-1) earlier in the season 24–14.

The Trojans huddle up in a 1980 game. As quarterback Gordon Adams (no. 2) calls the play, among those taking in the information is Roy Foster (no. 64), a two-time All-American (1980-81) and later a member of the Miami Dolphins and San Francisco 49ers, appearing in two Super Bowls.

The 1979 Trojans cheer from the sidelines. There was plenty to cheer about in a season in which the team went 11-0-1. That was part of a 28-game unbeaten streak that began after USC lost to Arizona State in 1978 and didn't end until the Trojans were defeated by Washington in 1980.

This was a tough day for USC. Leading Stanford 21–0 at the Coliseum in 1979 in front of 76,067, the Trojans were unable to halt a second-half Stanford rally that resulted in a 21–21 tie. That was the only blot on USC's otherwise perfect season.

This was a much better day for the Trojans. The week after the 1979 Stanford game, USC faced another challenge, Notre Dame at South Bend in front of a capacity crowd of 59,075. The Trojans came into the game ranked fourth, Notre Dame at number 9. USC regained the momentum lost a week earlier with a 45–23 triumph.

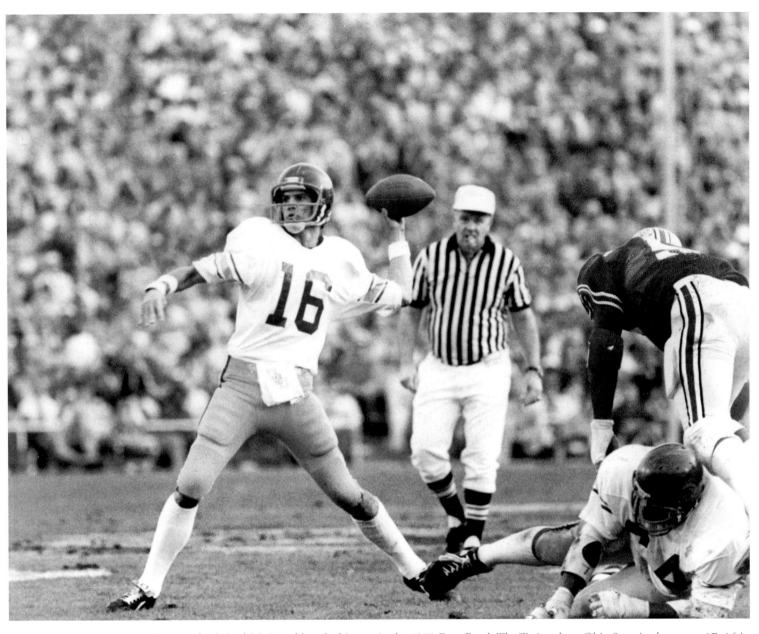

USC quarterback Paul McDonald cocks his arm in the 1980 Rose Bowl. The Trojans beat Ohio State in that game 17–16 in front of 105,526. McDonald, an All-American that season, was a Trojan from 1977 to 1979. He played in the NFL with the Cleveland Browns and Dallas Cowboys and is now the radio analyst on USC football broadcasts.

NOTES ON THE PHOTOGRAPHS

These notes, listed by page number, attempt to include all aspects known of the photographs. Each of the photographs is identified by the page number, photograph's title or description, photographer and collection, archive, and call or box number when applicable. Although every attempt was made to collect all data, in some cases complete data may have been unavailable due to the age and condition of some of the photographs and records.

II   **USC SQUAD FOR 1905**
USC
1905football-031

VI   **RUGBY MATCH AGAINST
MANUAL ARTS, 1913**
USC
1913football-13-
11rugbyvsmanualarts1913-
034

X   **FIRST OFFICIAL
FOOTBALL TEAM**
USC
1888football-1888team-029

2   **COACH LEWIS FREEMAN
WITH TEAM, 1897**
USC
oldfootball-varsity1897-003

3   **THE TEAM A YEAR
LATER**
USC
oldfootball-1898team-026

4   **USC RUGBY TEAM**
USC
oldfootball-1911-1913-028

5   **RUGBY TEAM FOR 1912**
USC
1912football-varsitysquad-
032

6   **RUGBY TEAM FOR 1913**
USC
1913football-13-57pharmacy
football1913-033

7   **USC VS. CALIFORNIA,
1913**
USC
1913football-13-
41vsberkeley1913-036

8   **RUGBY TEAM IN ACTION**
USC
1913football-17-
1613vsstmarys1913-035

9   **USC VS. LAAC, 1914**
USC
1914football-14-
232vsLACC1914-039

10   **USC VS. LAAC NO. 2**
USC
oldfootball-14-161-022

11   **USC VS. REDLANDS,
1914**
USC
1914football-14-
248vsredlands1914-037

12   **USC VS. REDLANDS
NO. 2**
USC
1914football-14-
251vsredlands1914-038

13   **REVVING UP FOR THE
1915 SEASON**
USC
1915football-15-143-1915-045

14   **USC VS. LAAC AT THE
GOAL-LINE, 1915**
USC
1915football-15-
156vsLAHigh1915-041

15   **FINAL SEASON FOR
COACH RALPH GLAZE**
USC
1915football-15-
159vsLAAC1915-044

16   **THE TROJANS VS. ST.
MARY'S**
USC
1915football-15-170-
4vsstmarys1915-040

17   **USC VS. WHITTIER,
1915**
USC
1915football-15-
241vswhittier1915-043

200